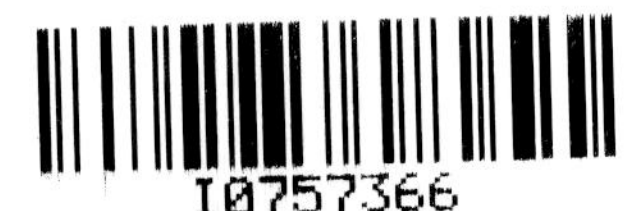

# Hand Drawn
# CHIBI GIRLS
## Kids Coloring Book

## NINALARS

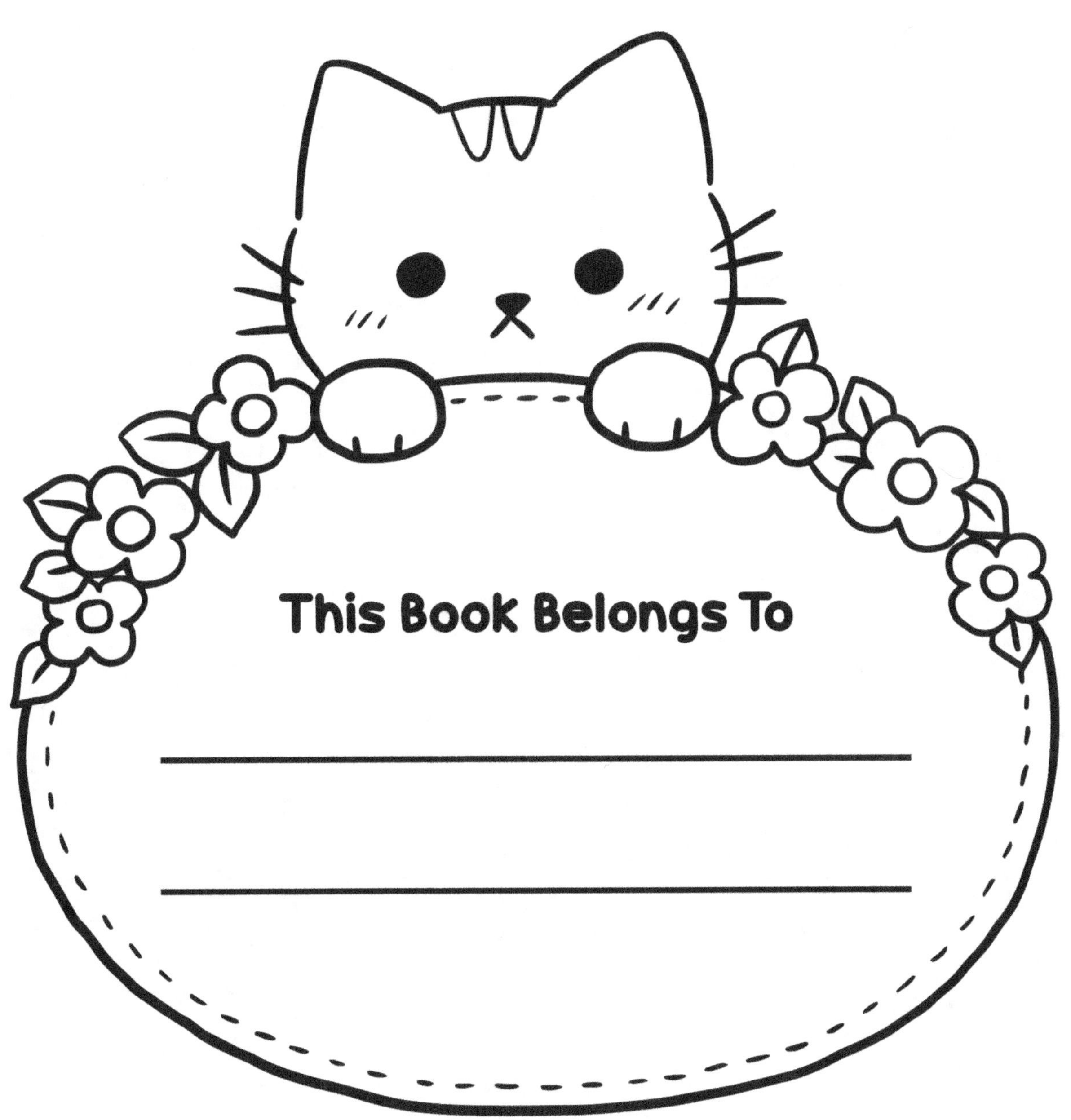

This Book Belongs To

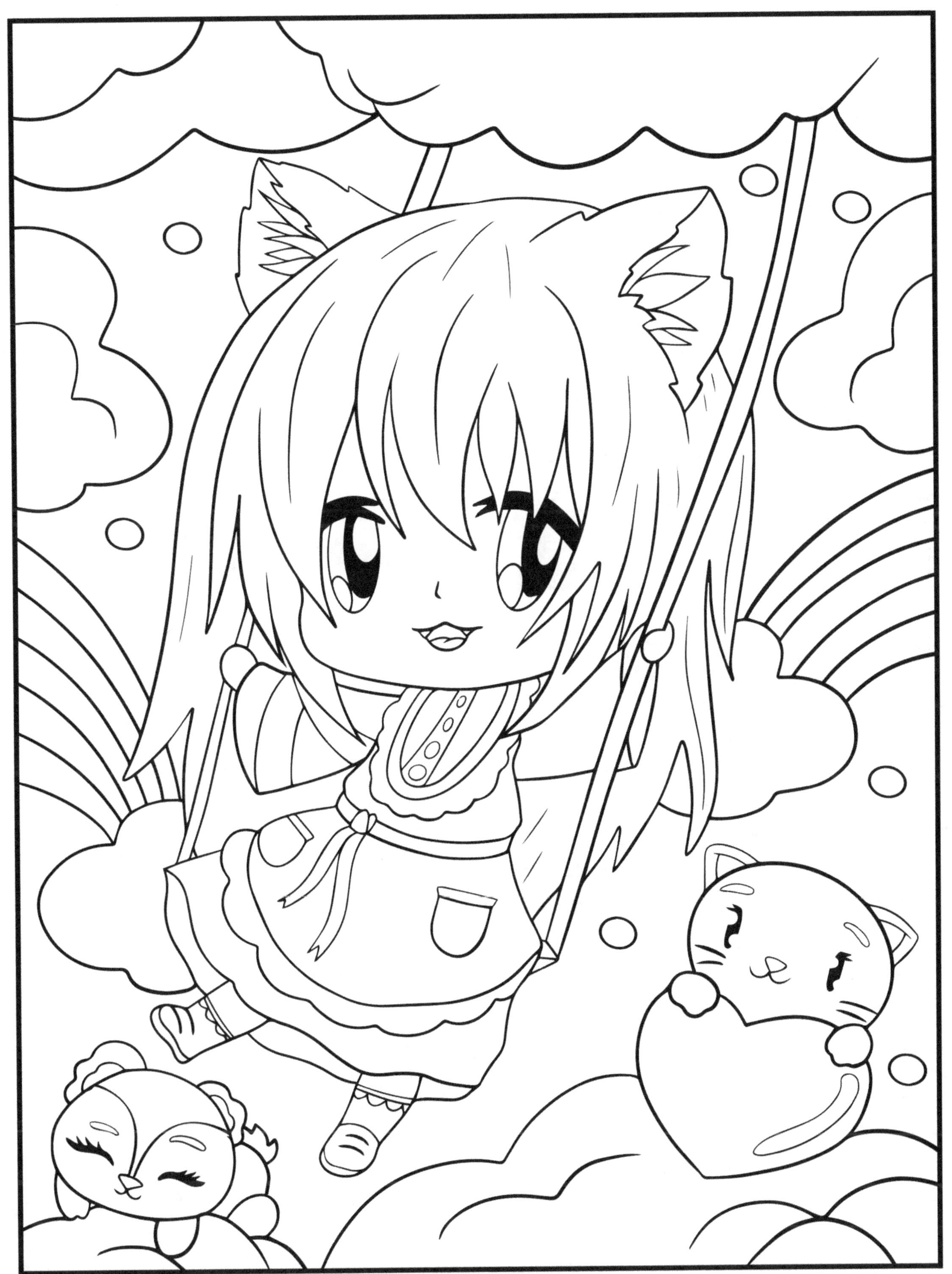

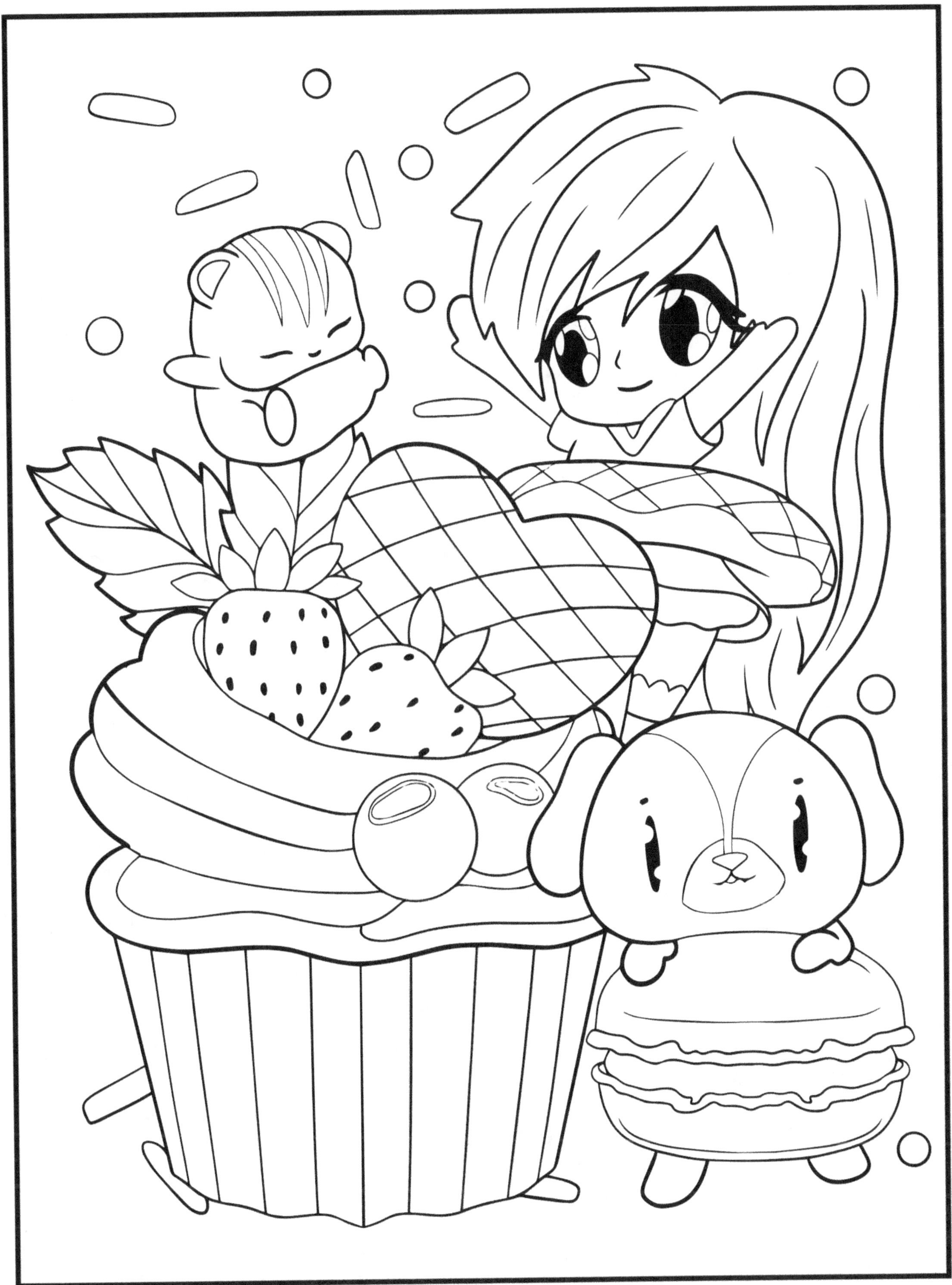

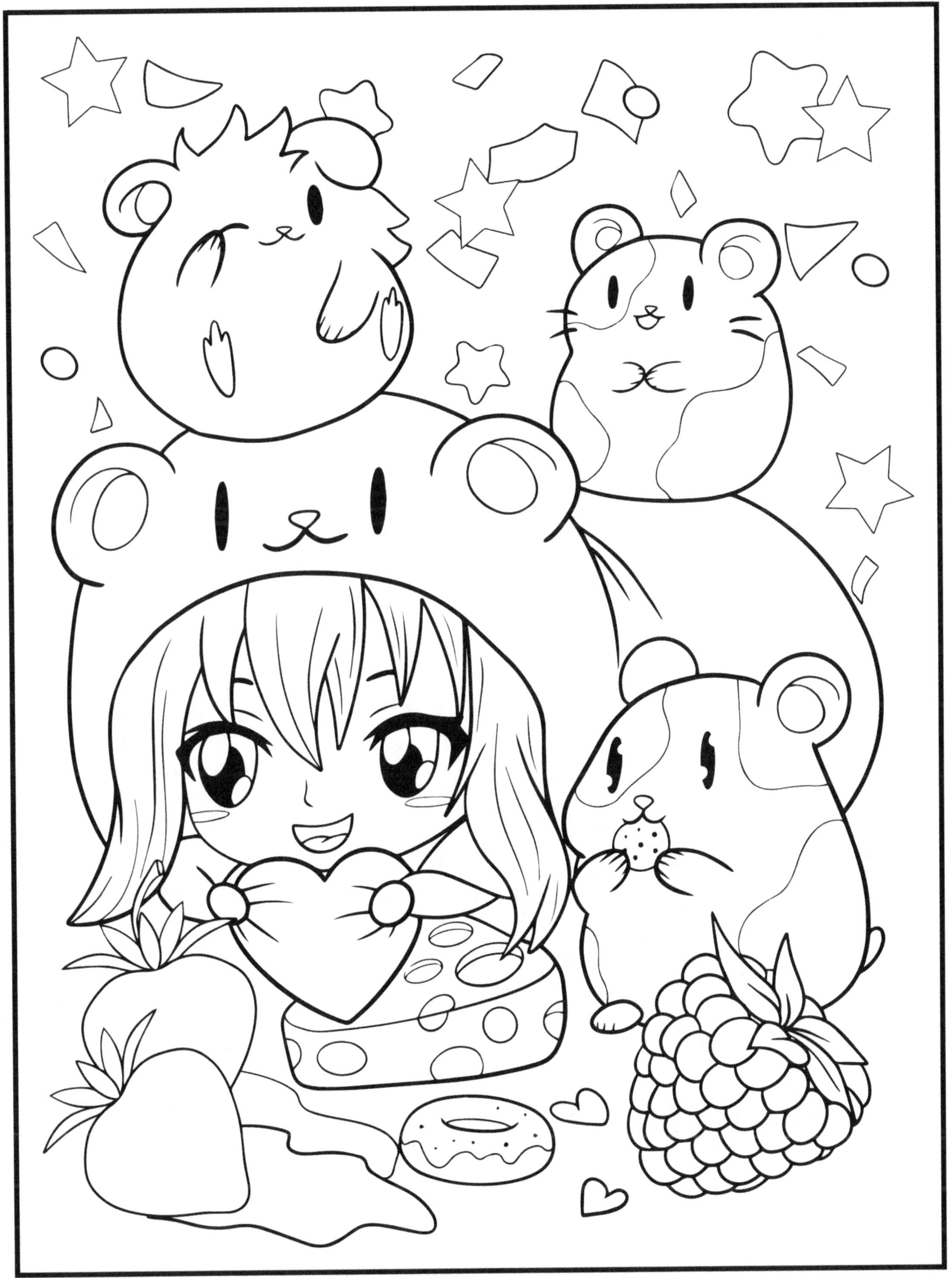

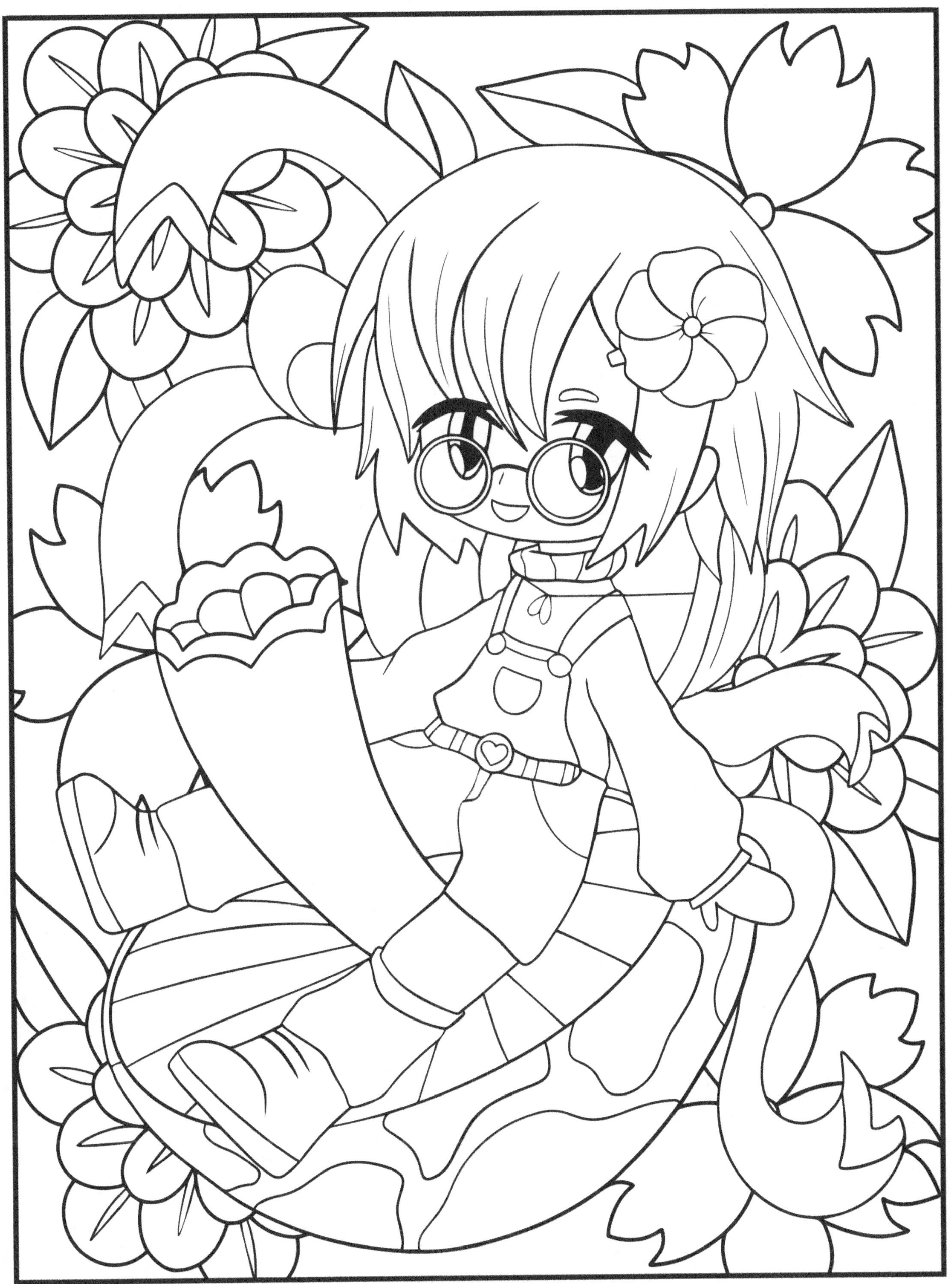

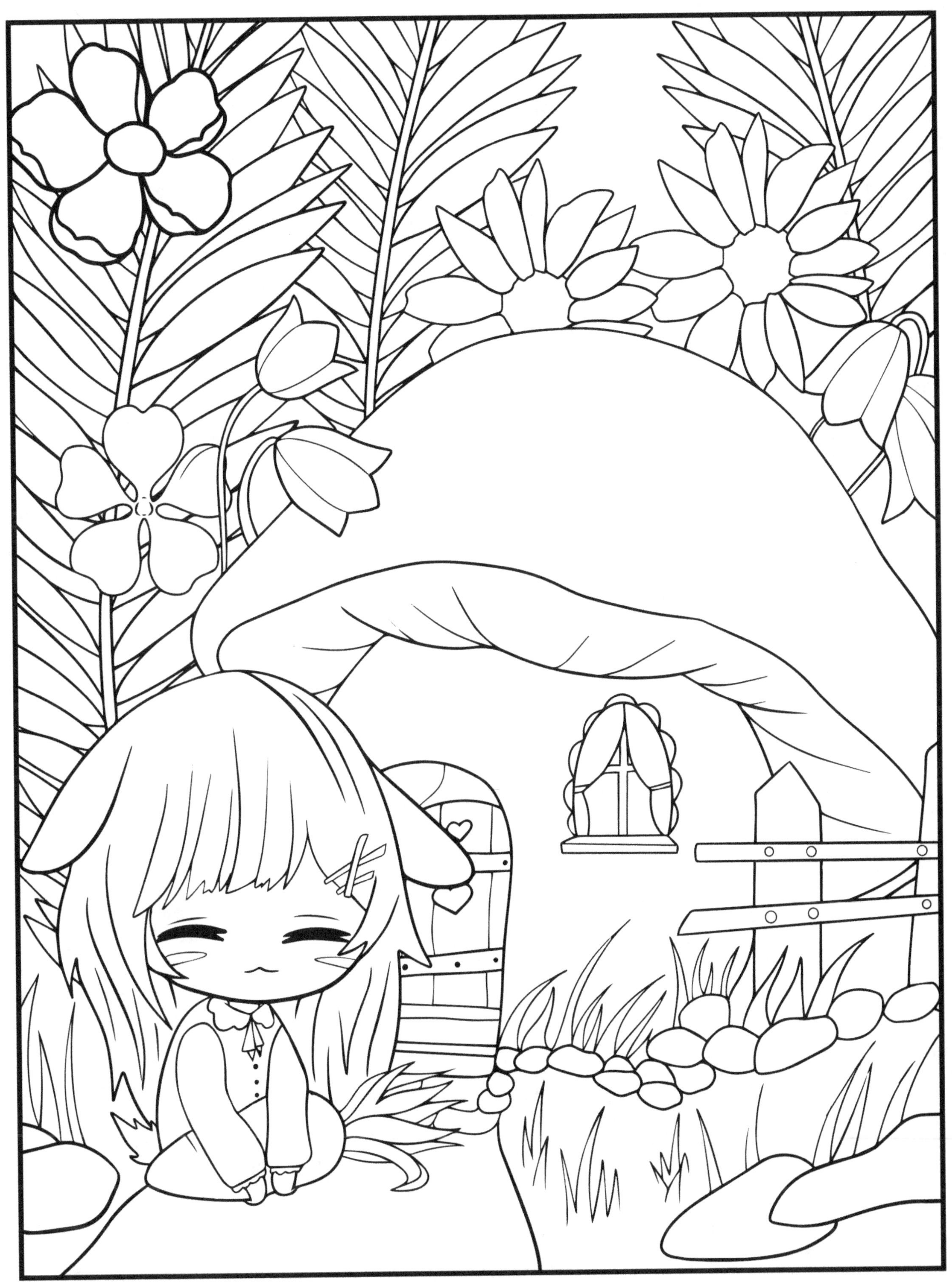

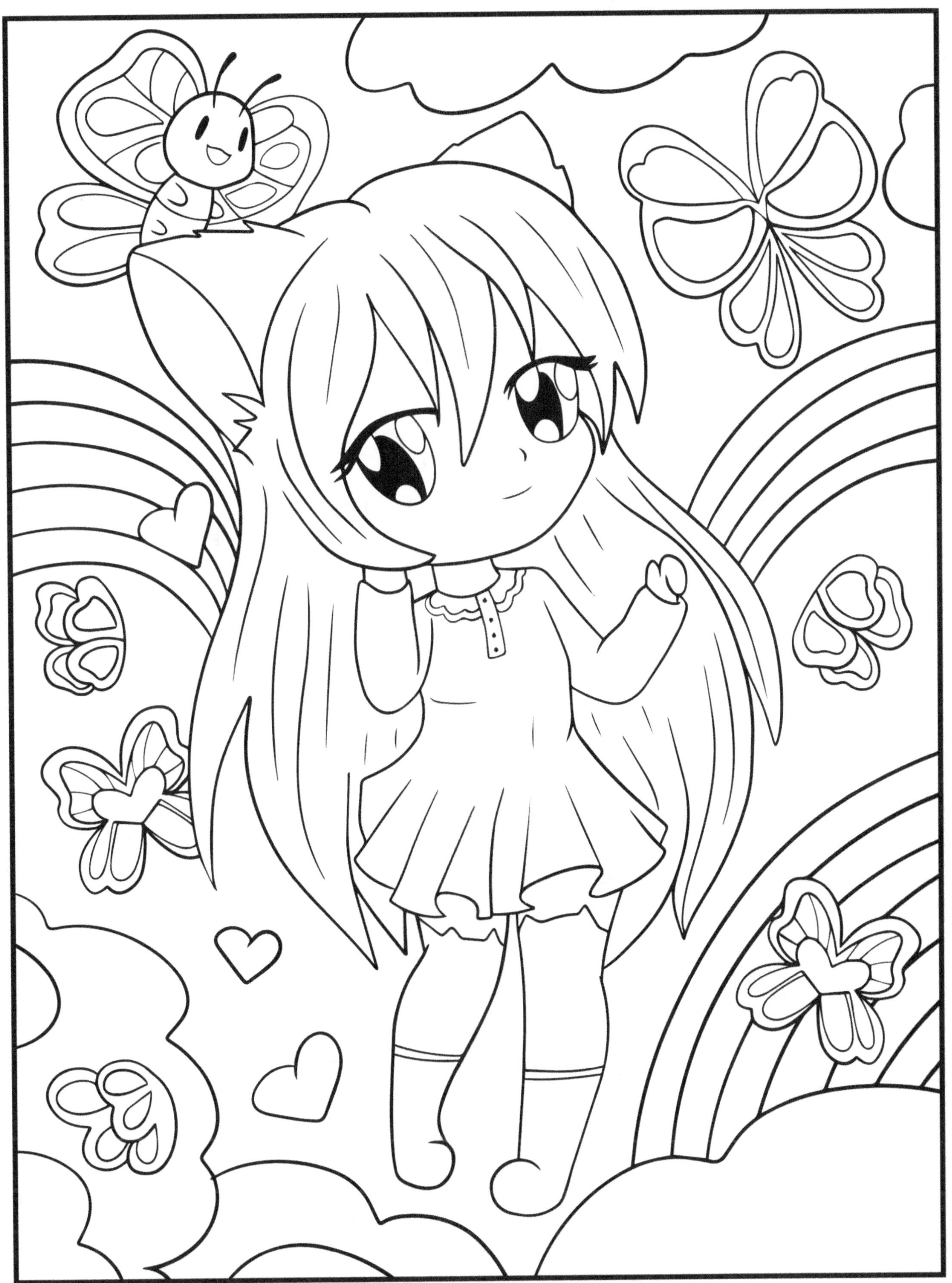

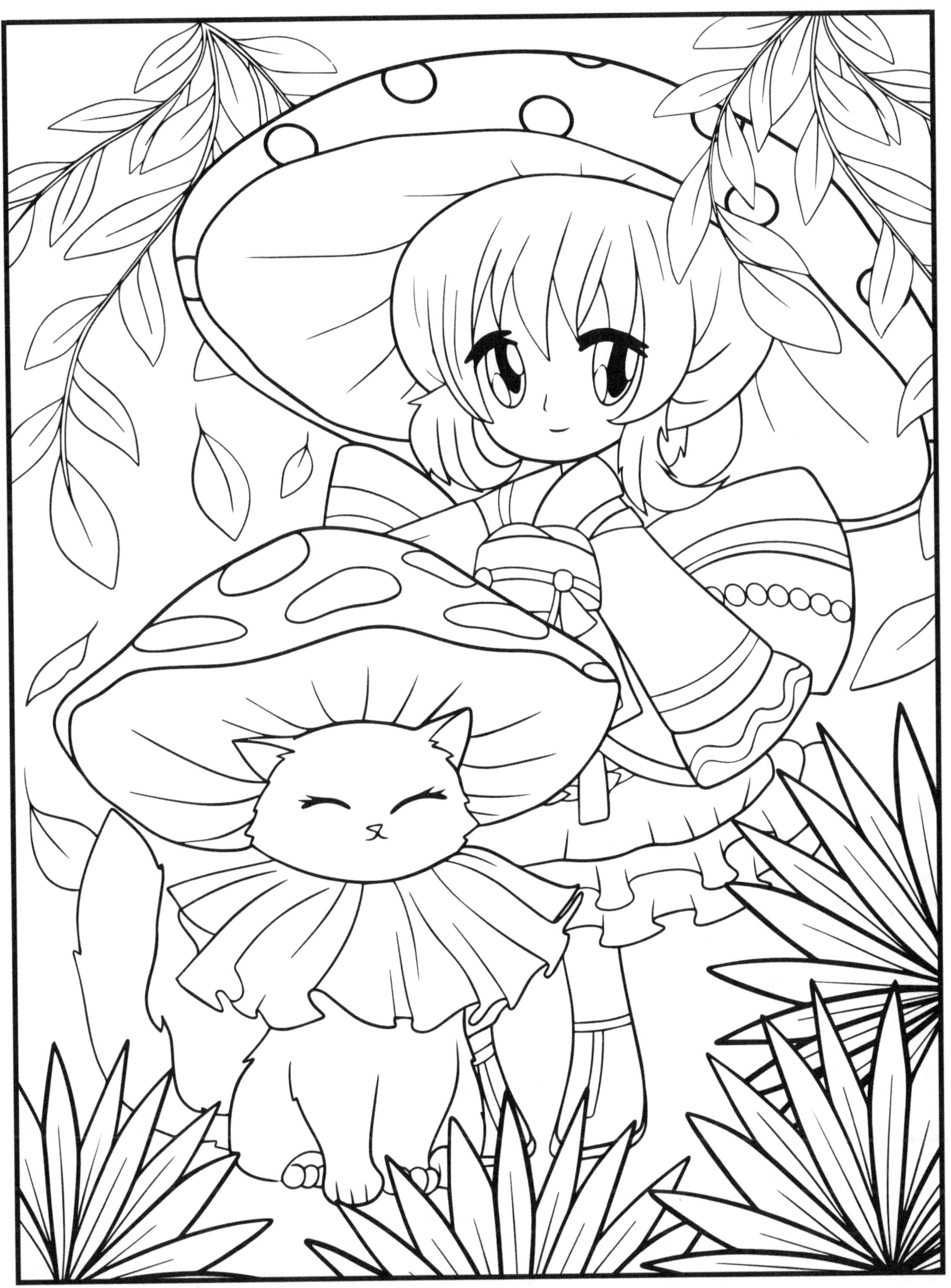

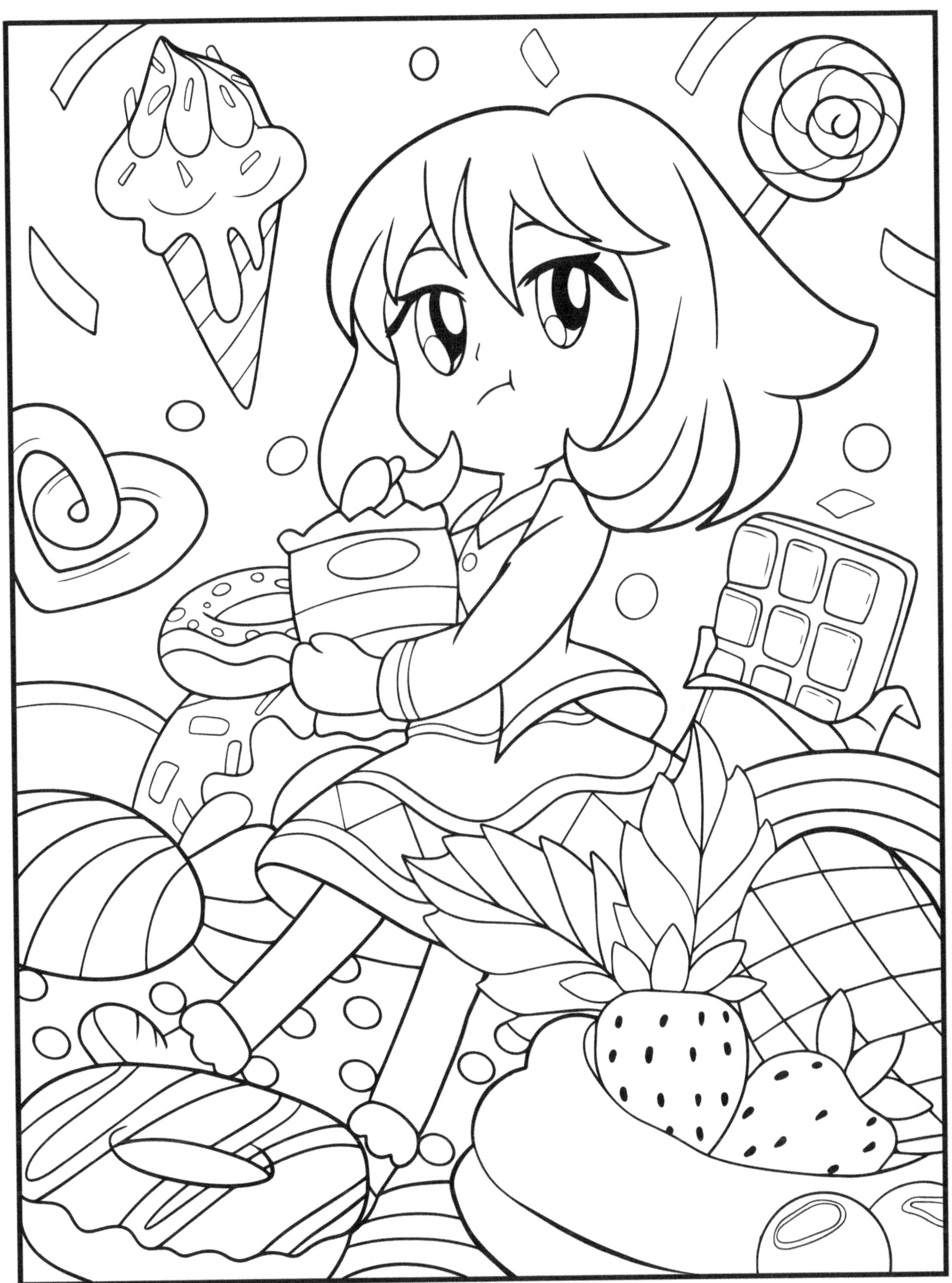

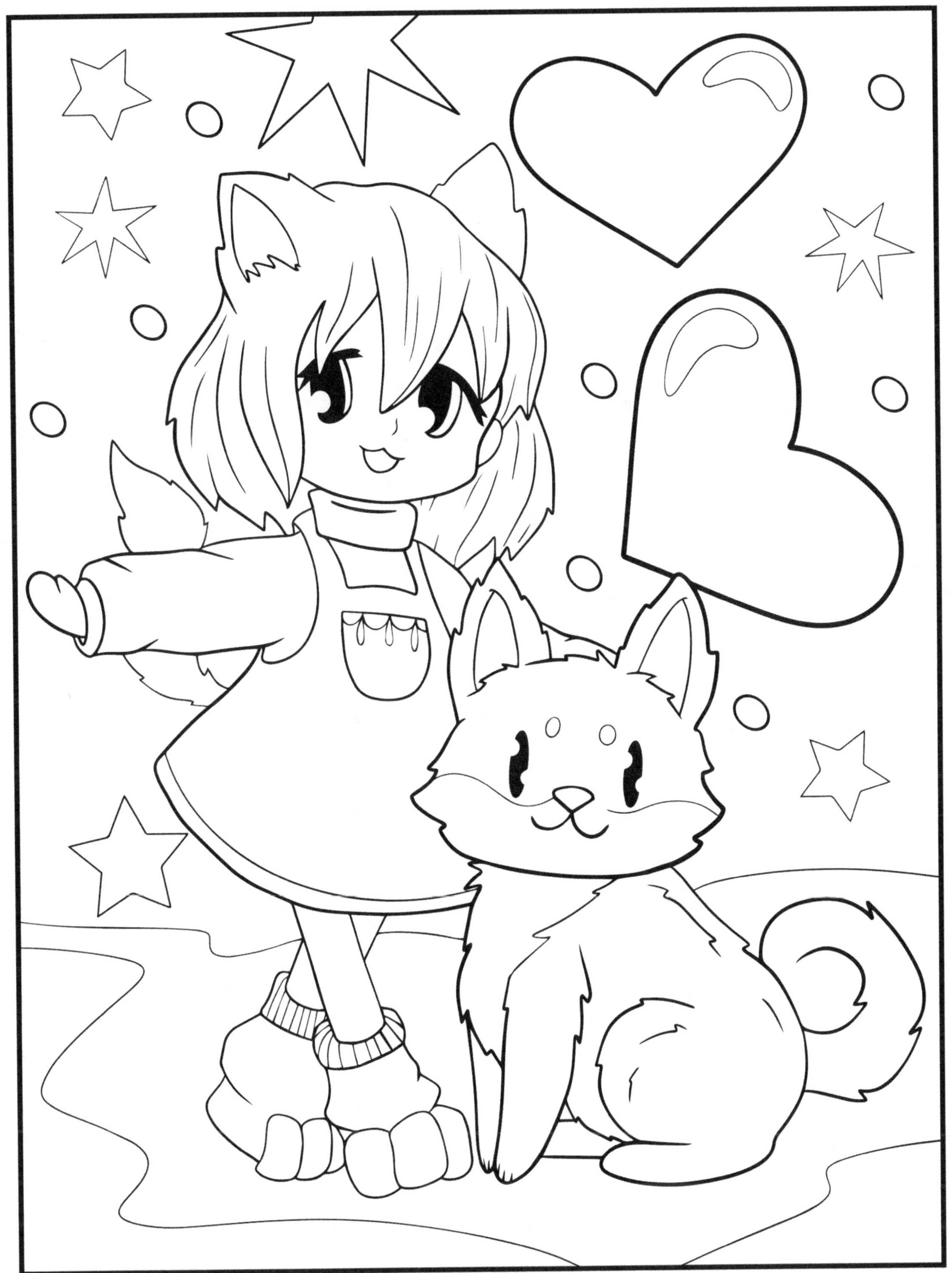

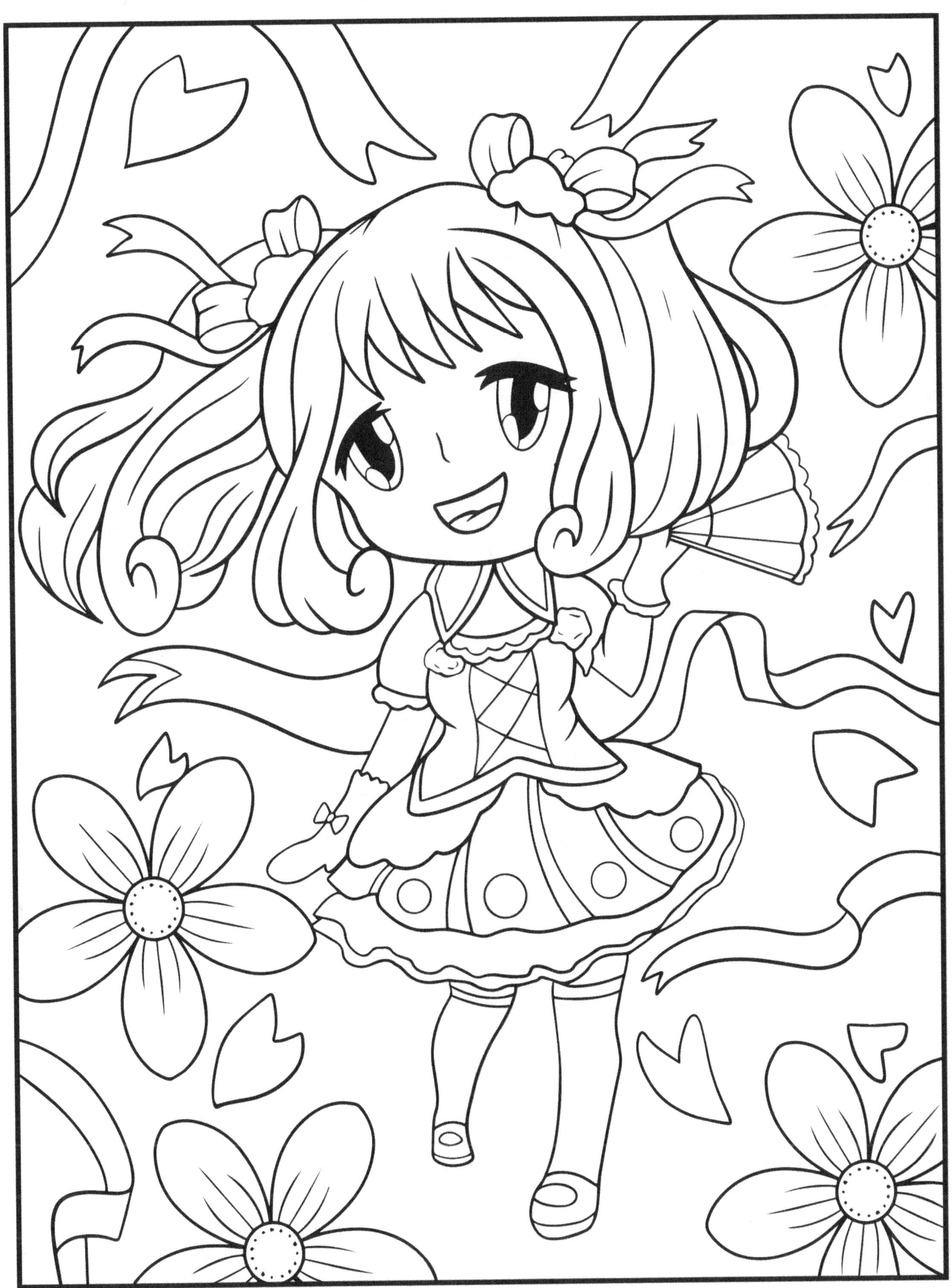

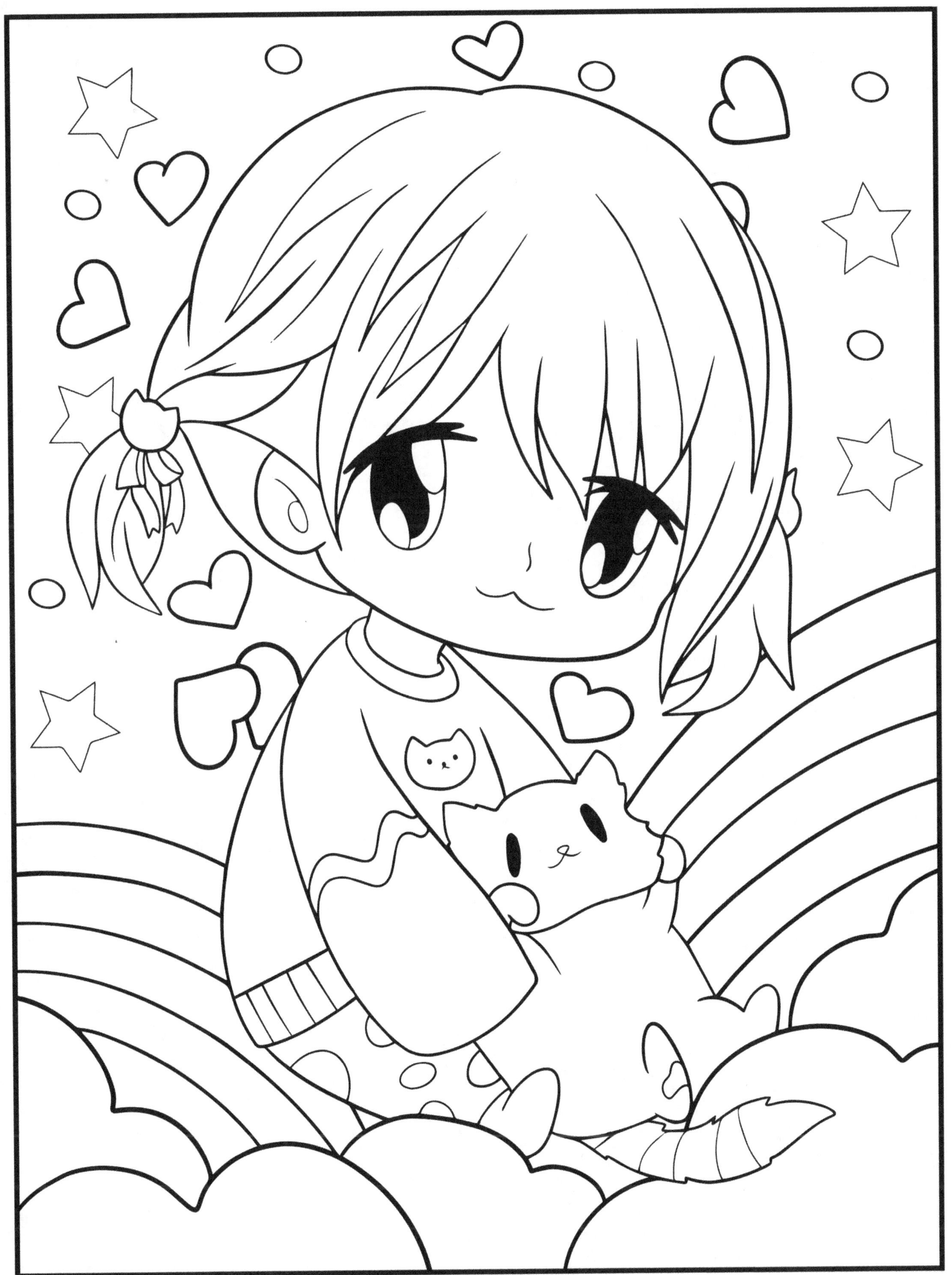

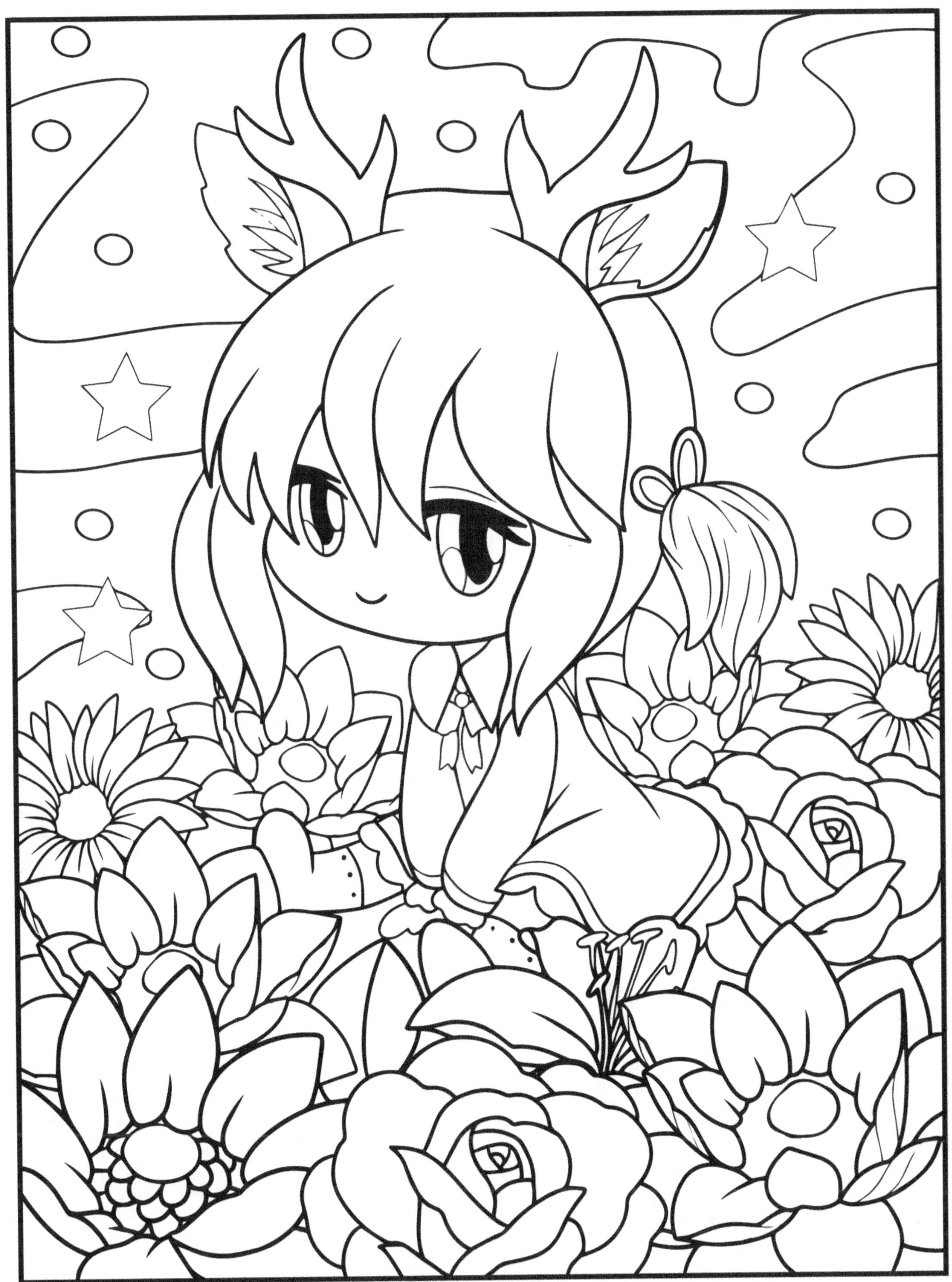

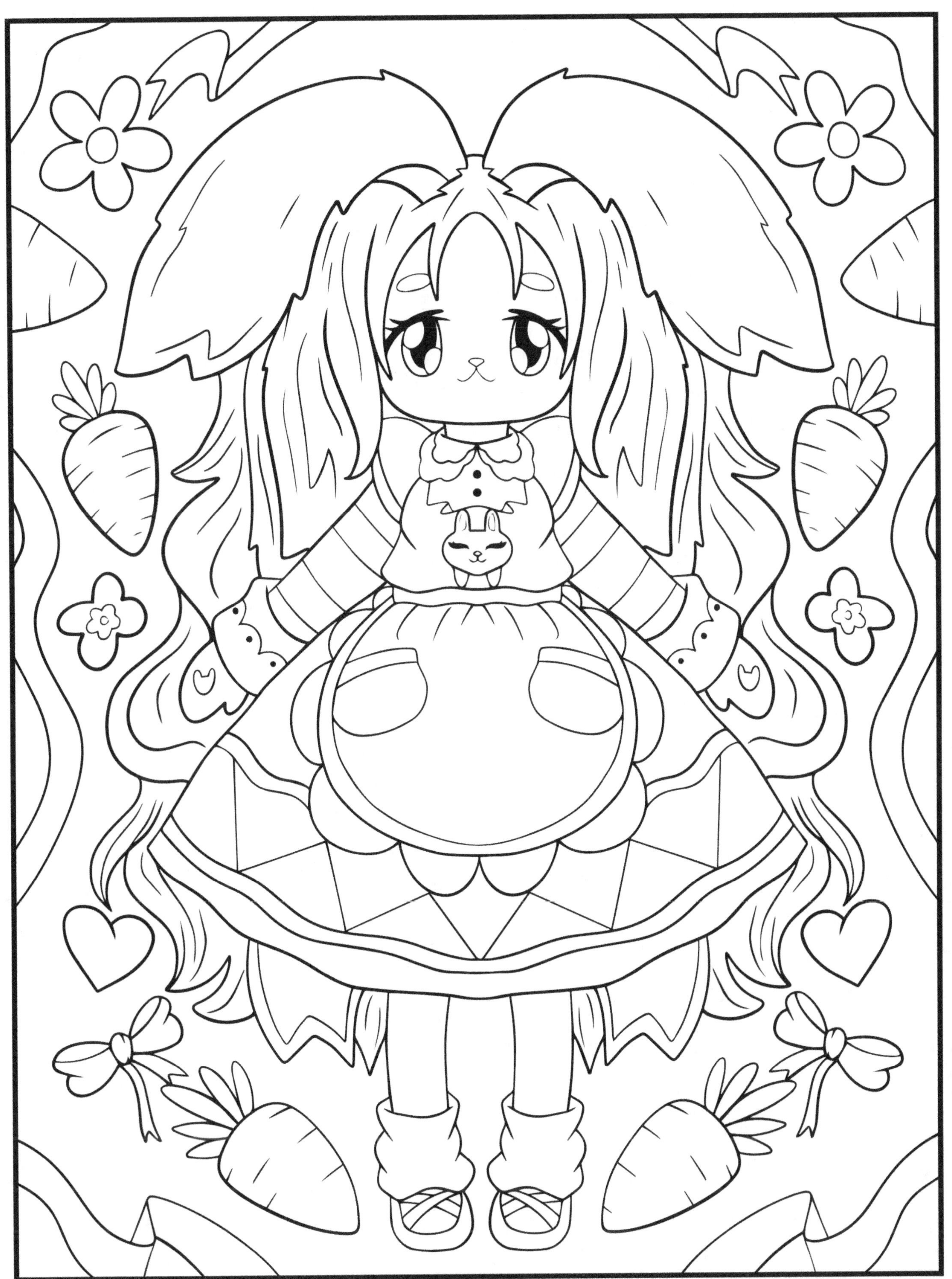

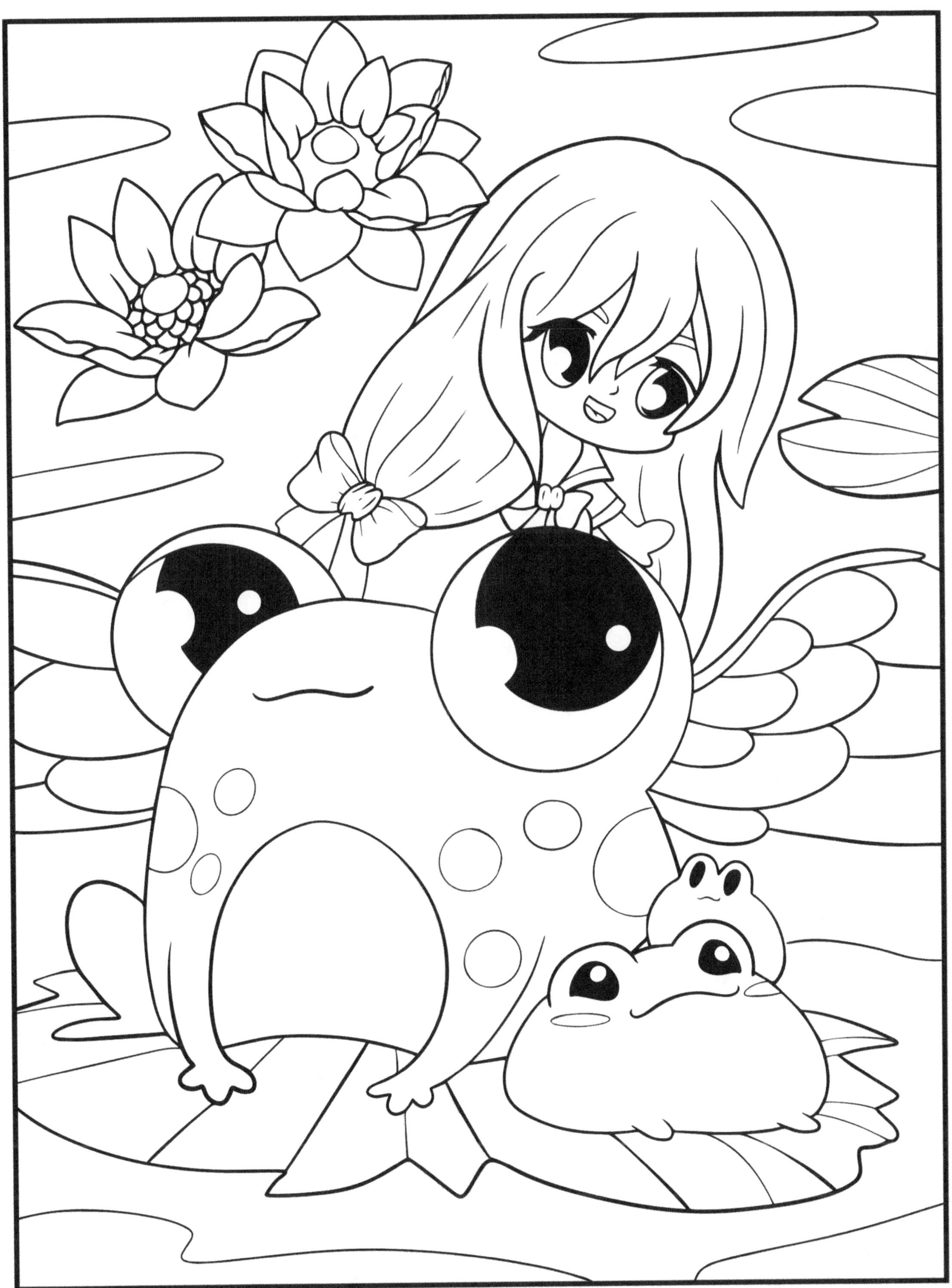

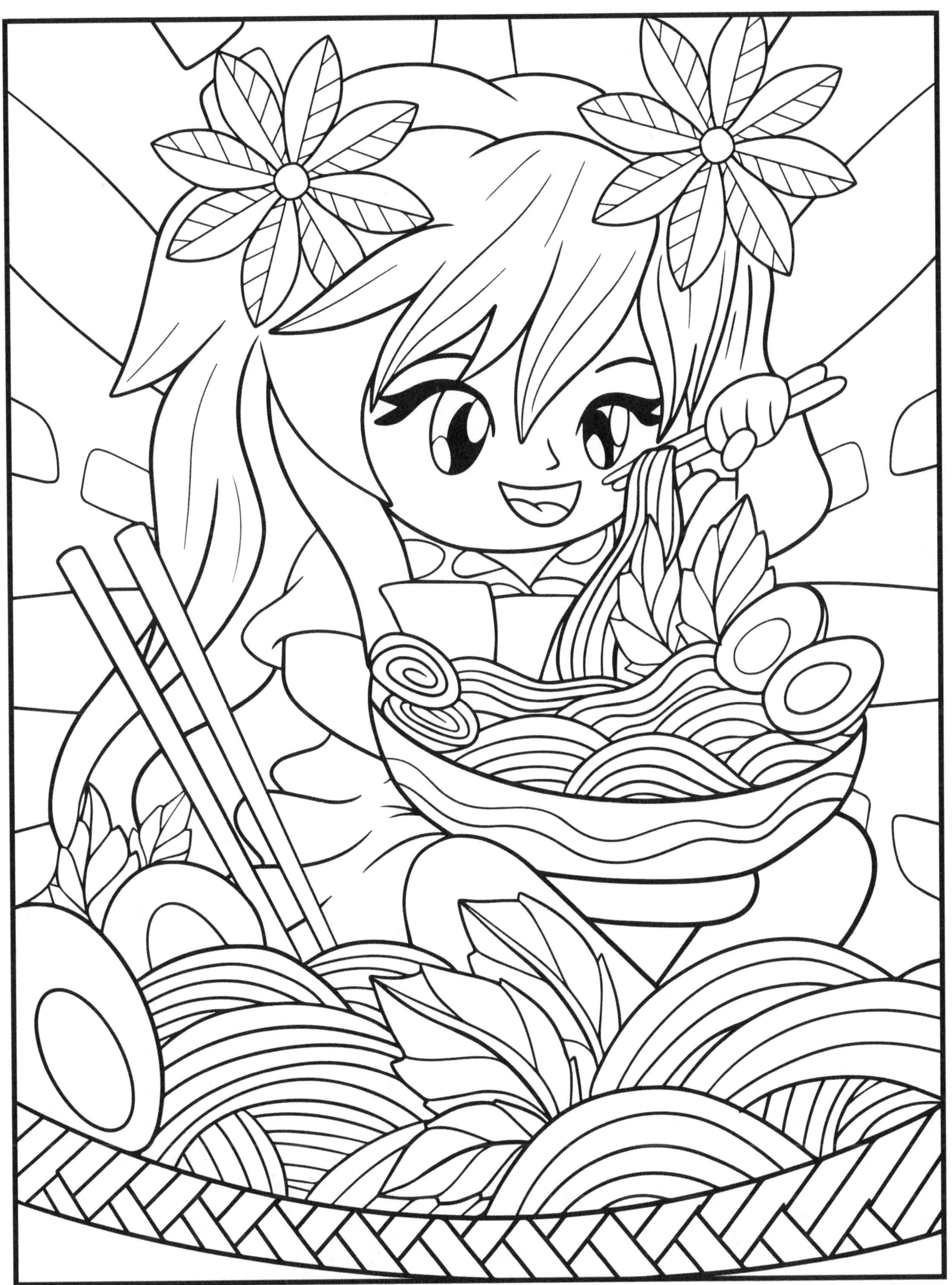

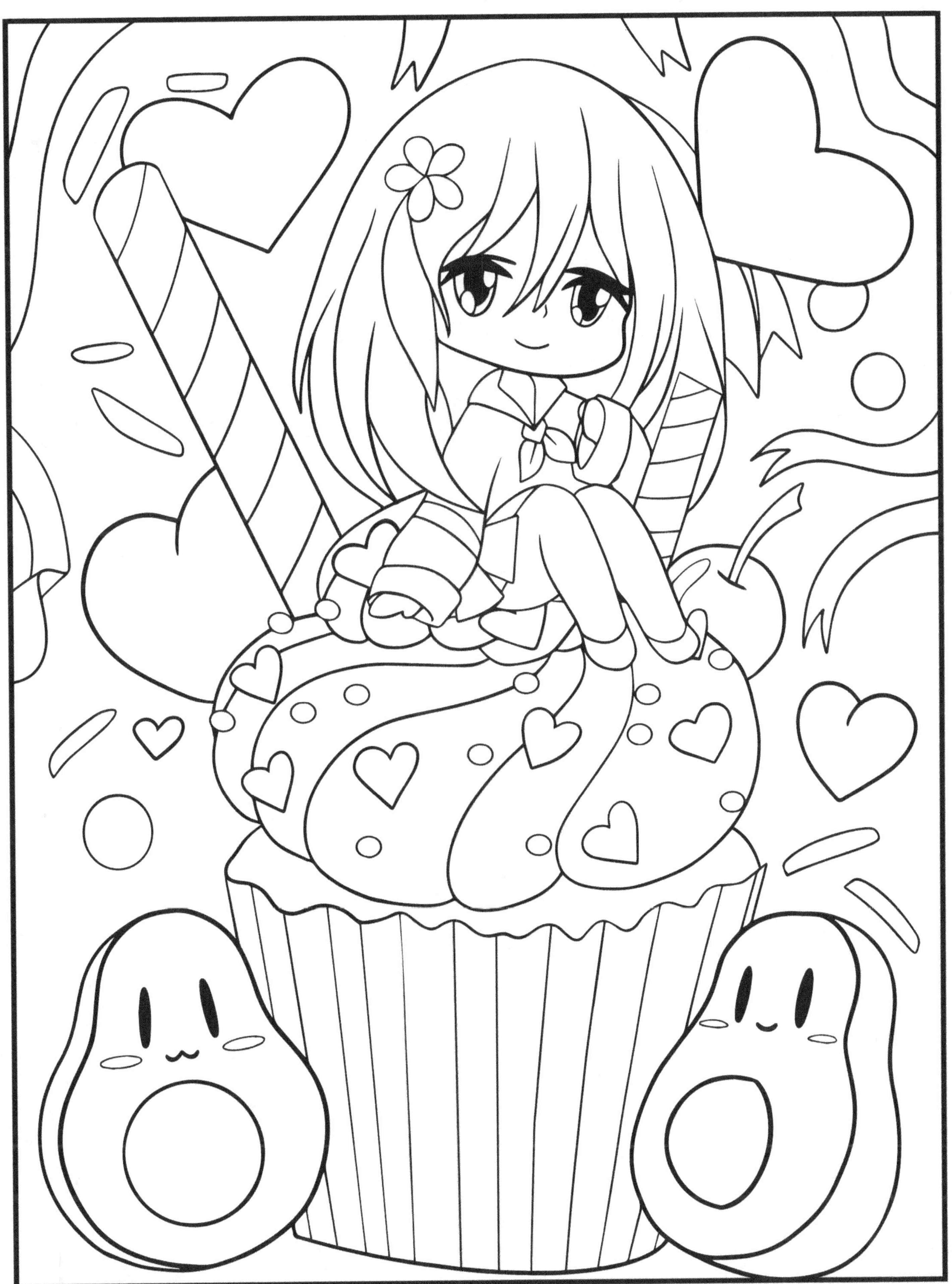

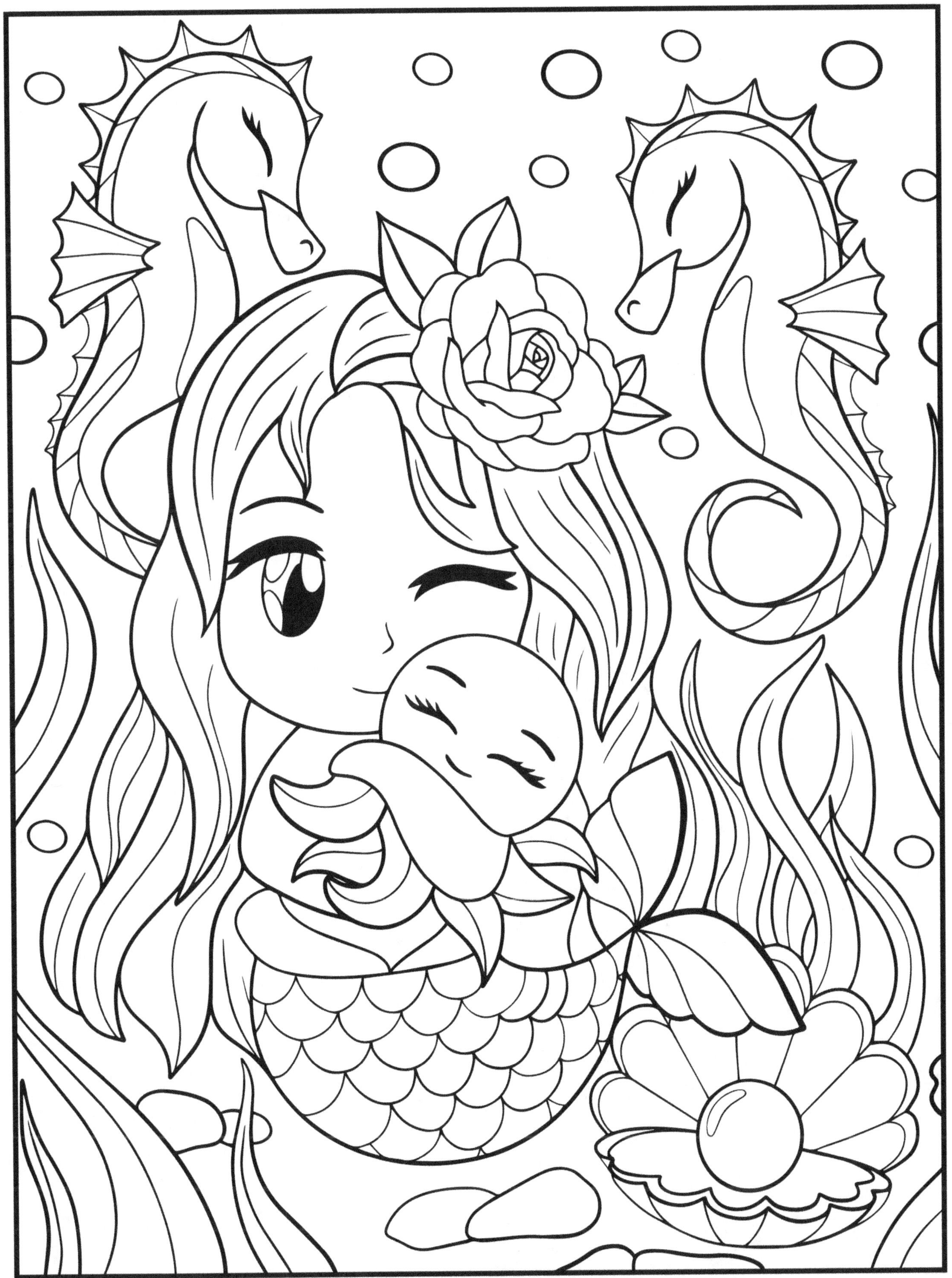

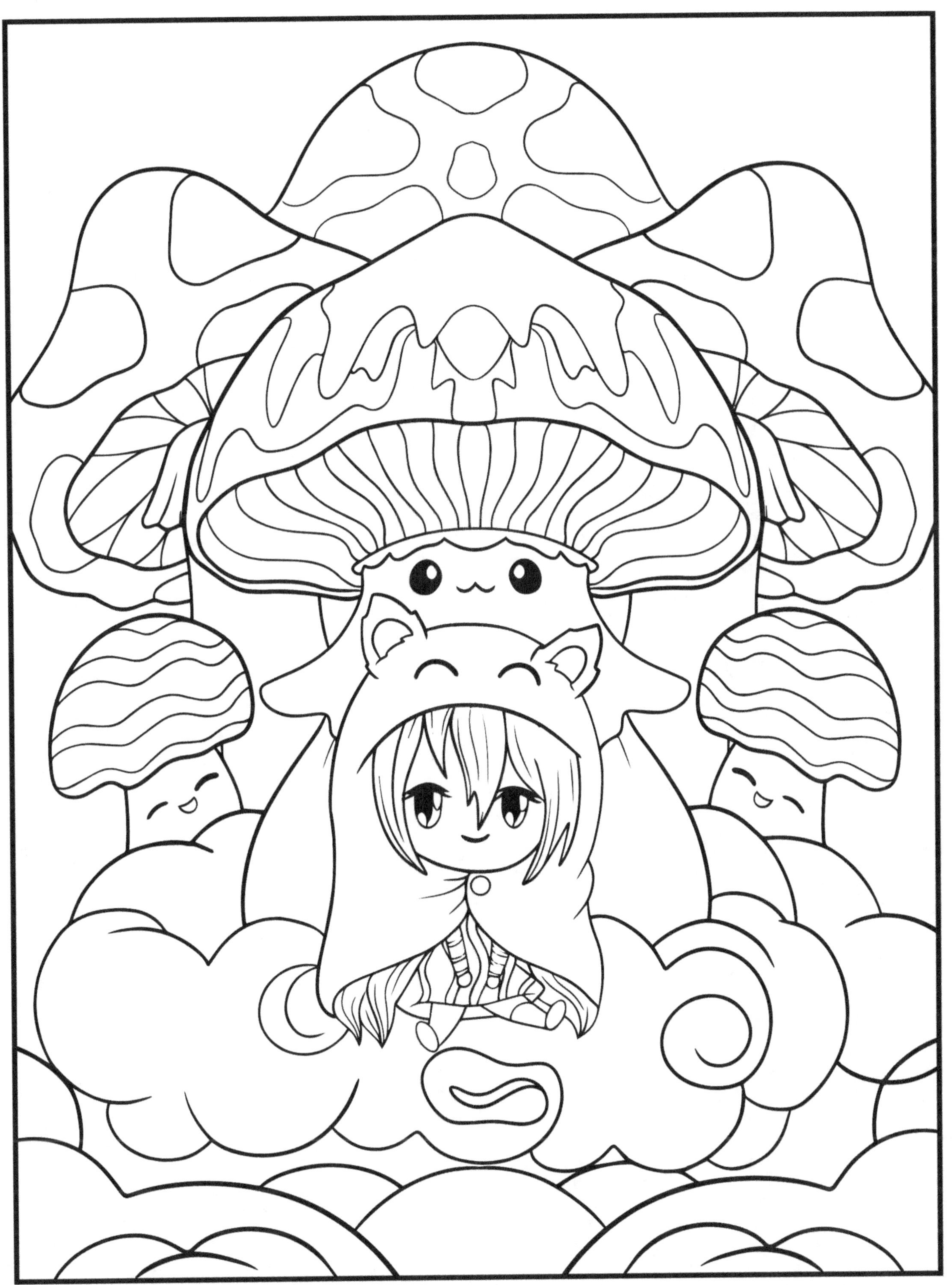

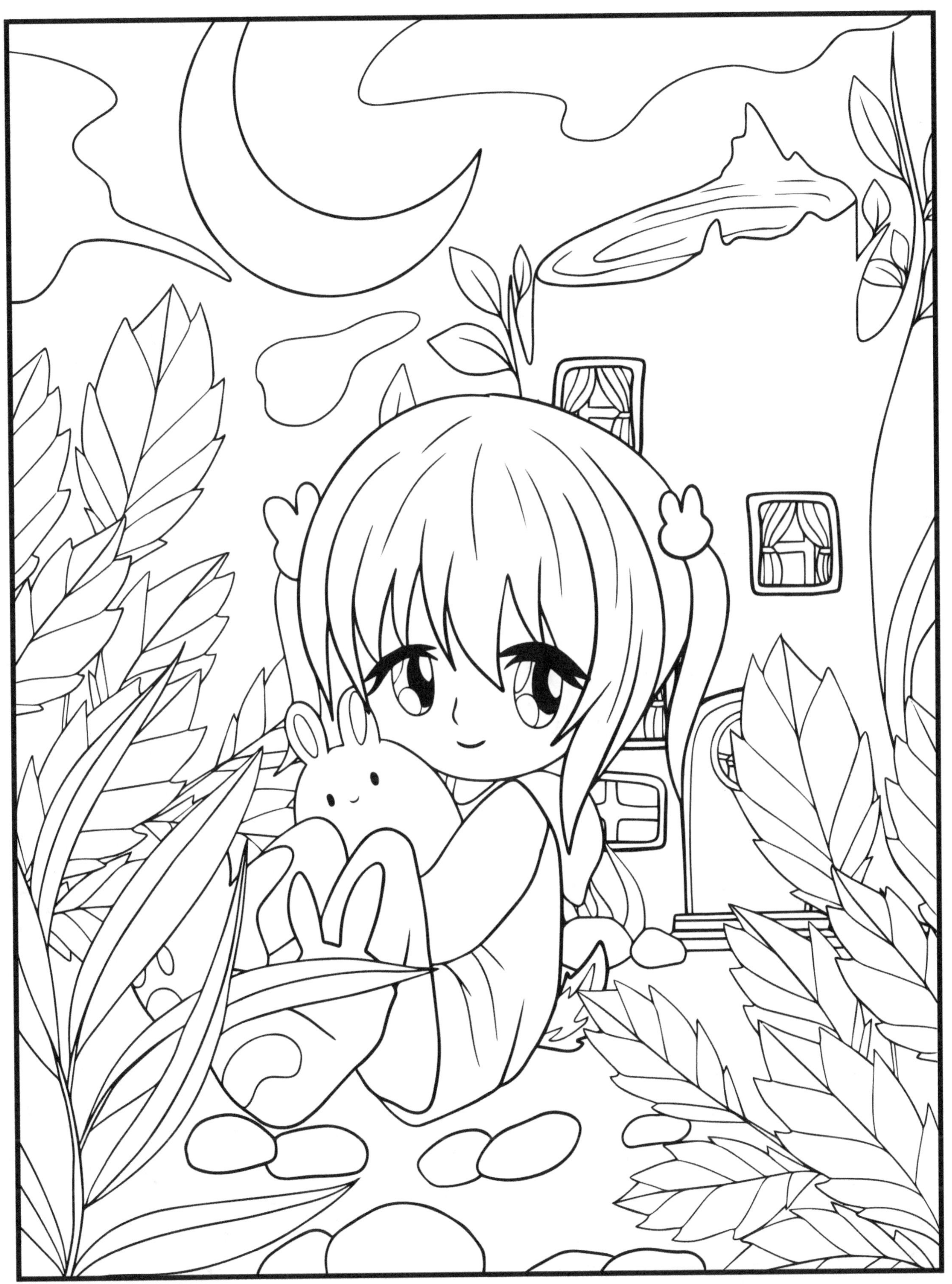

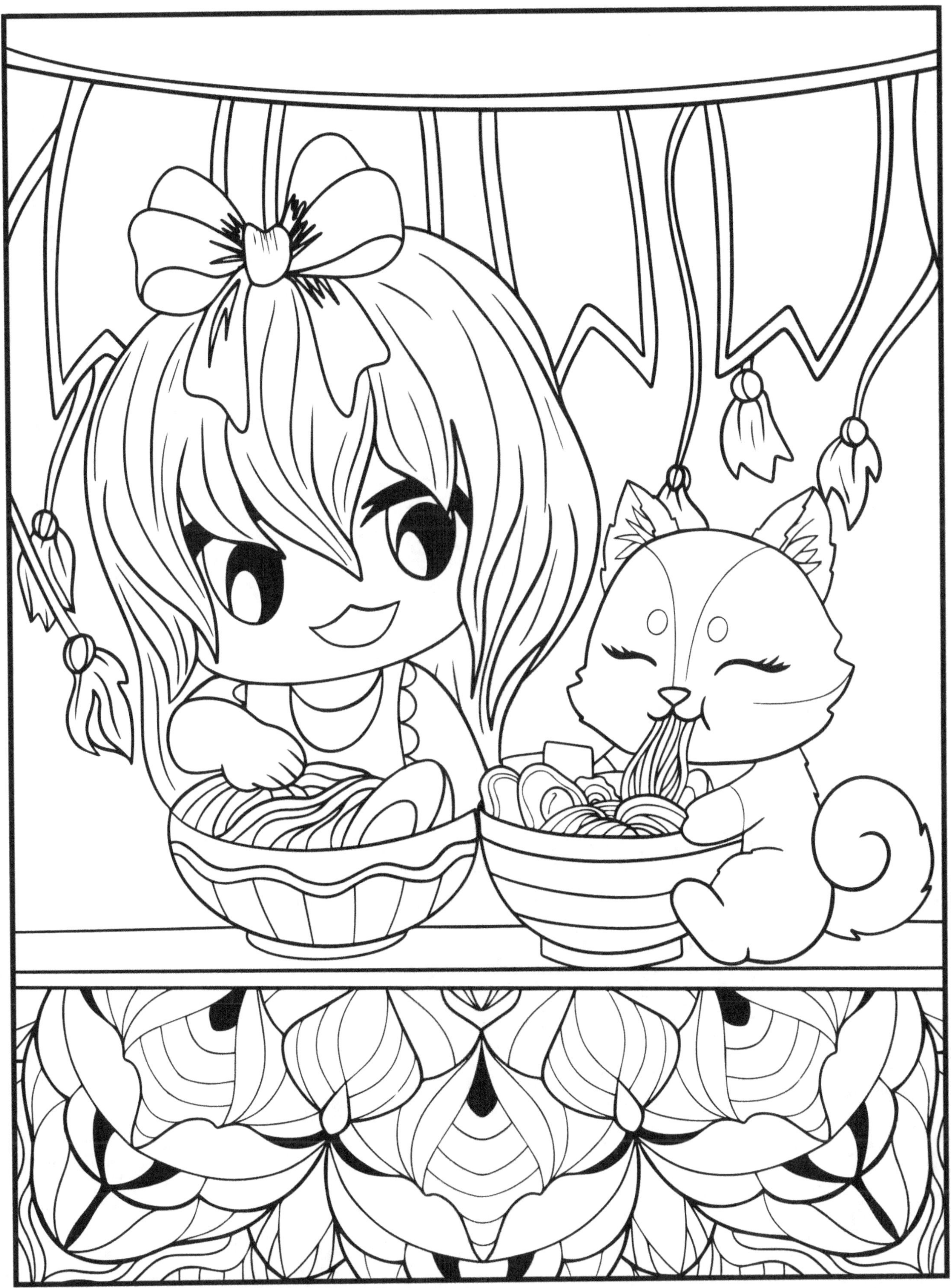

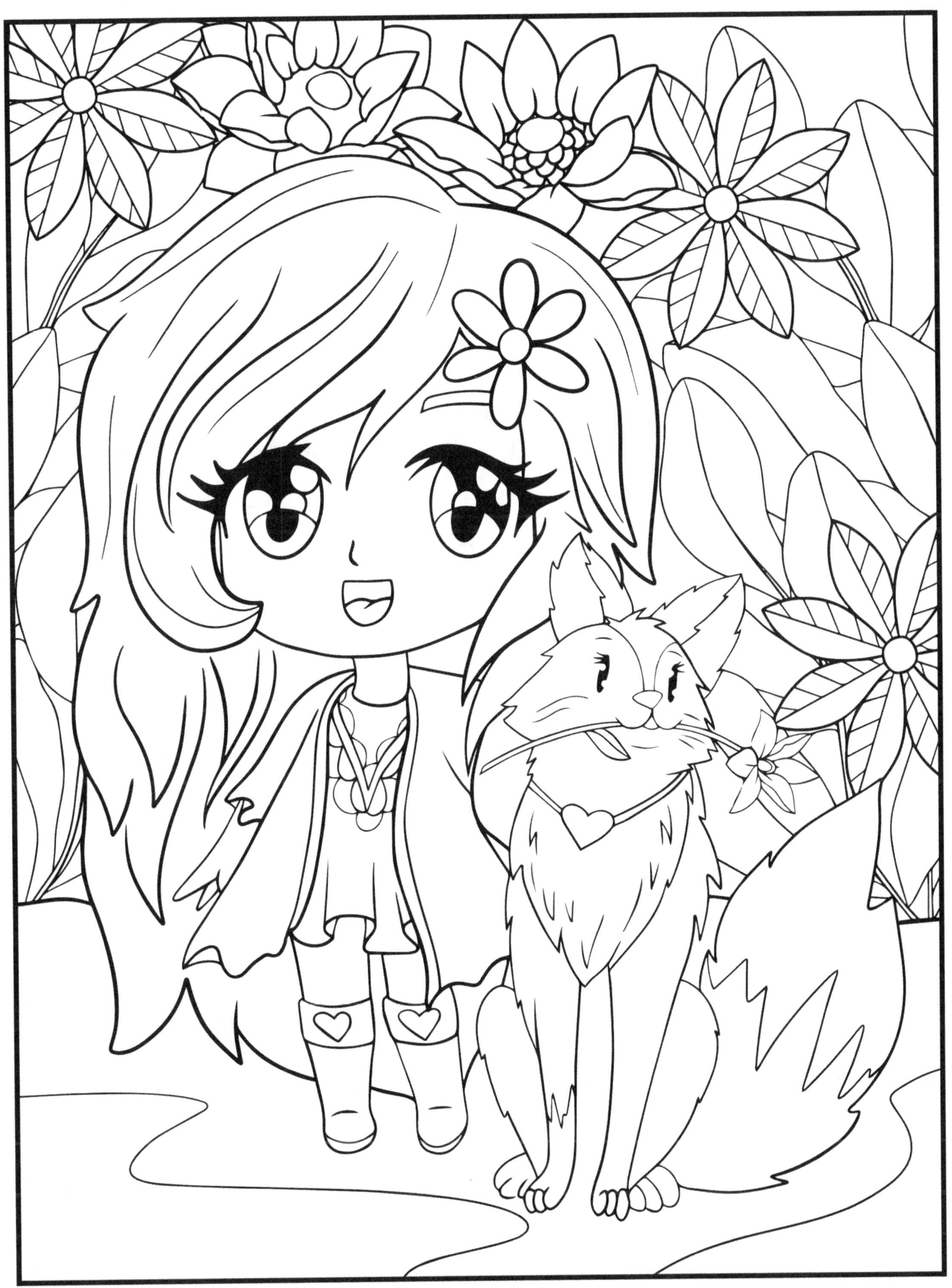

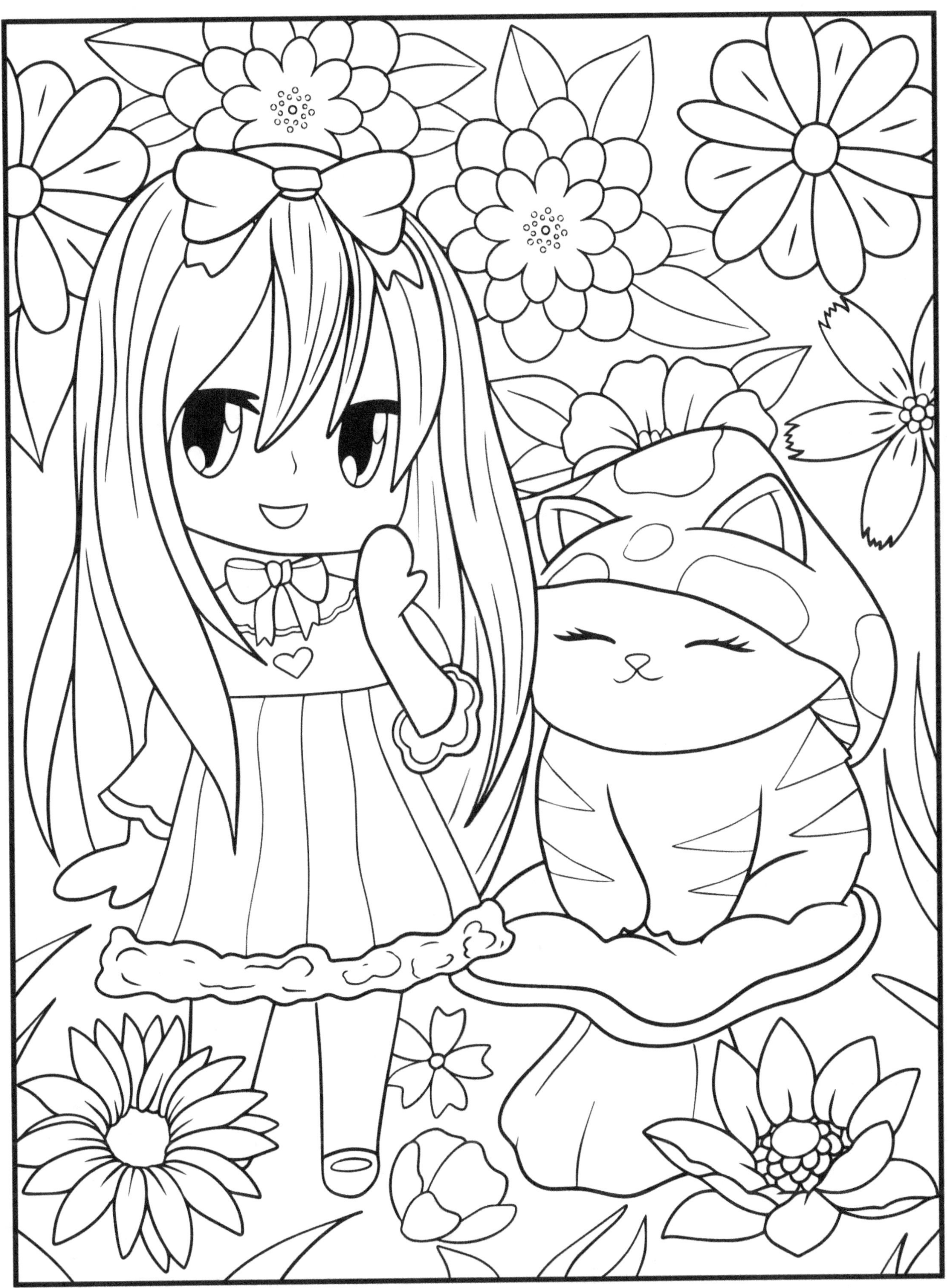

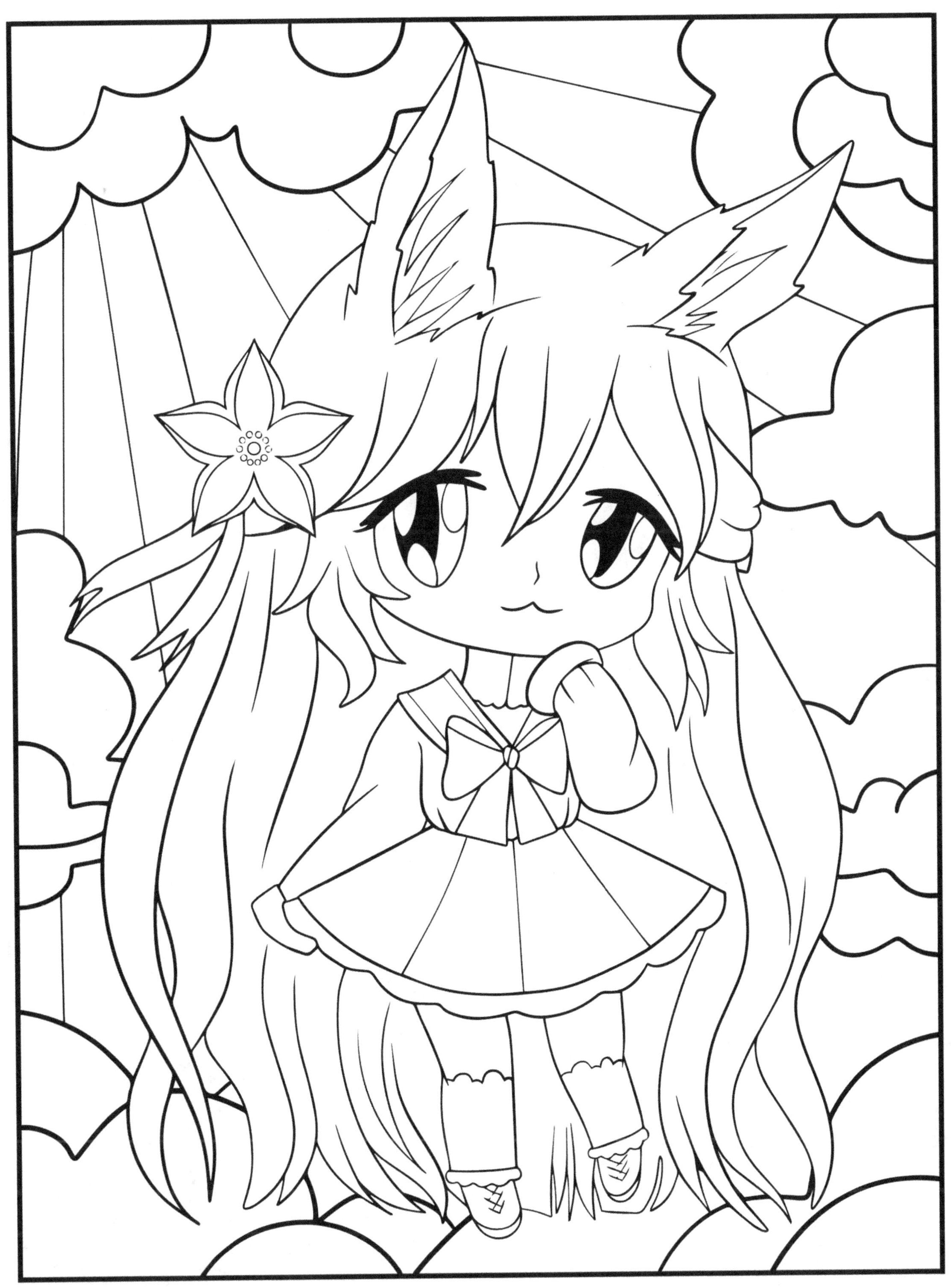

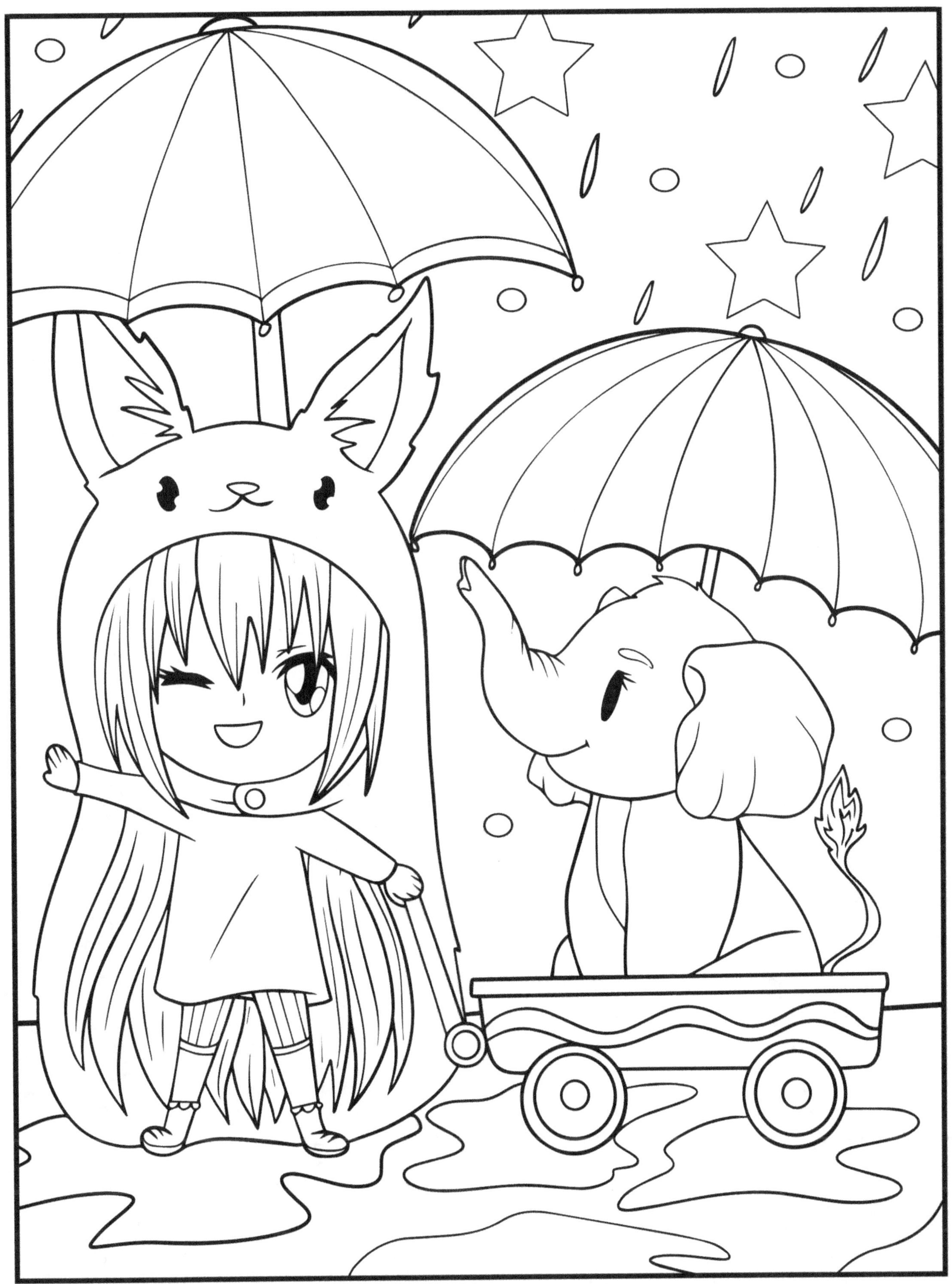

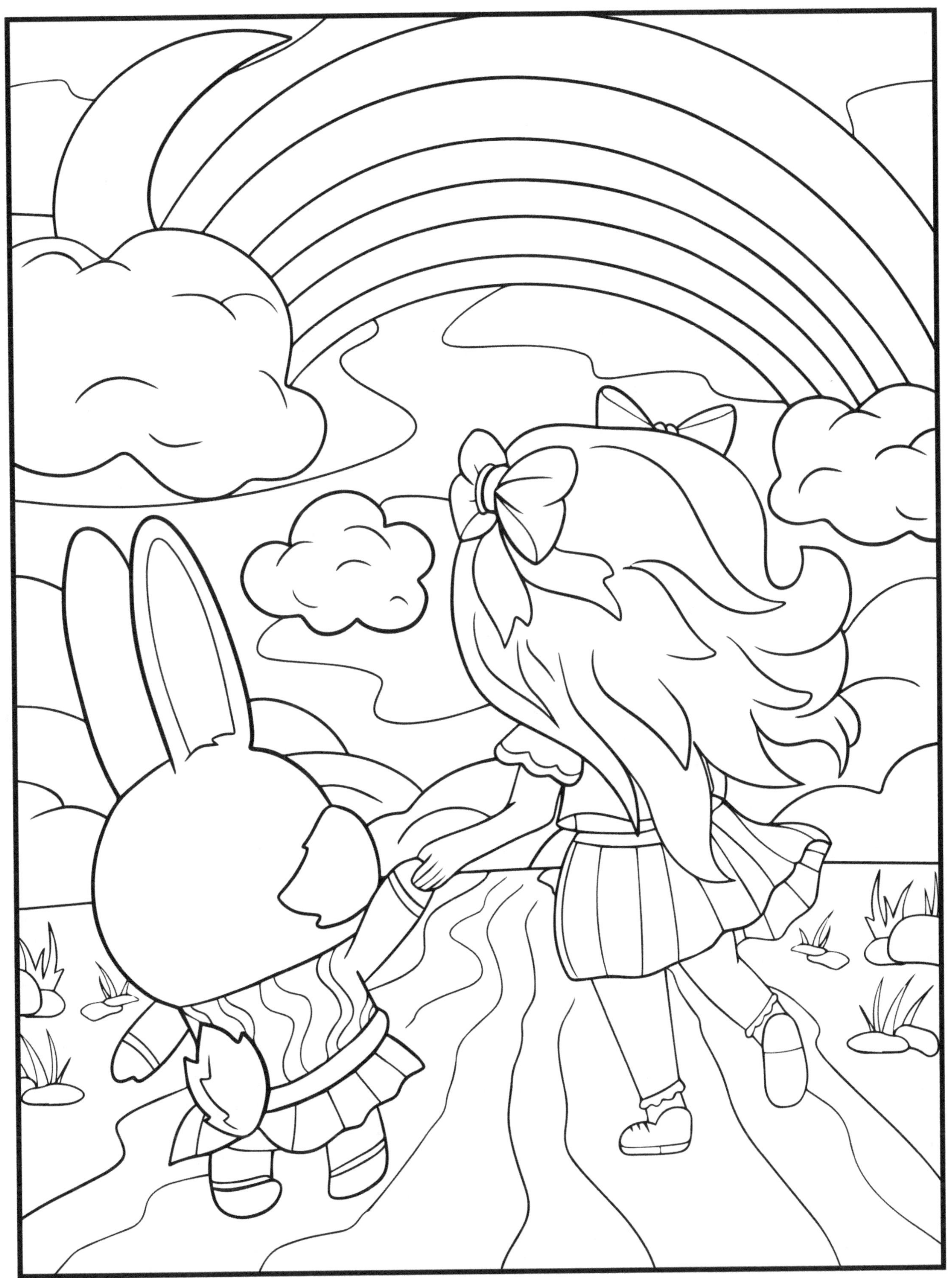

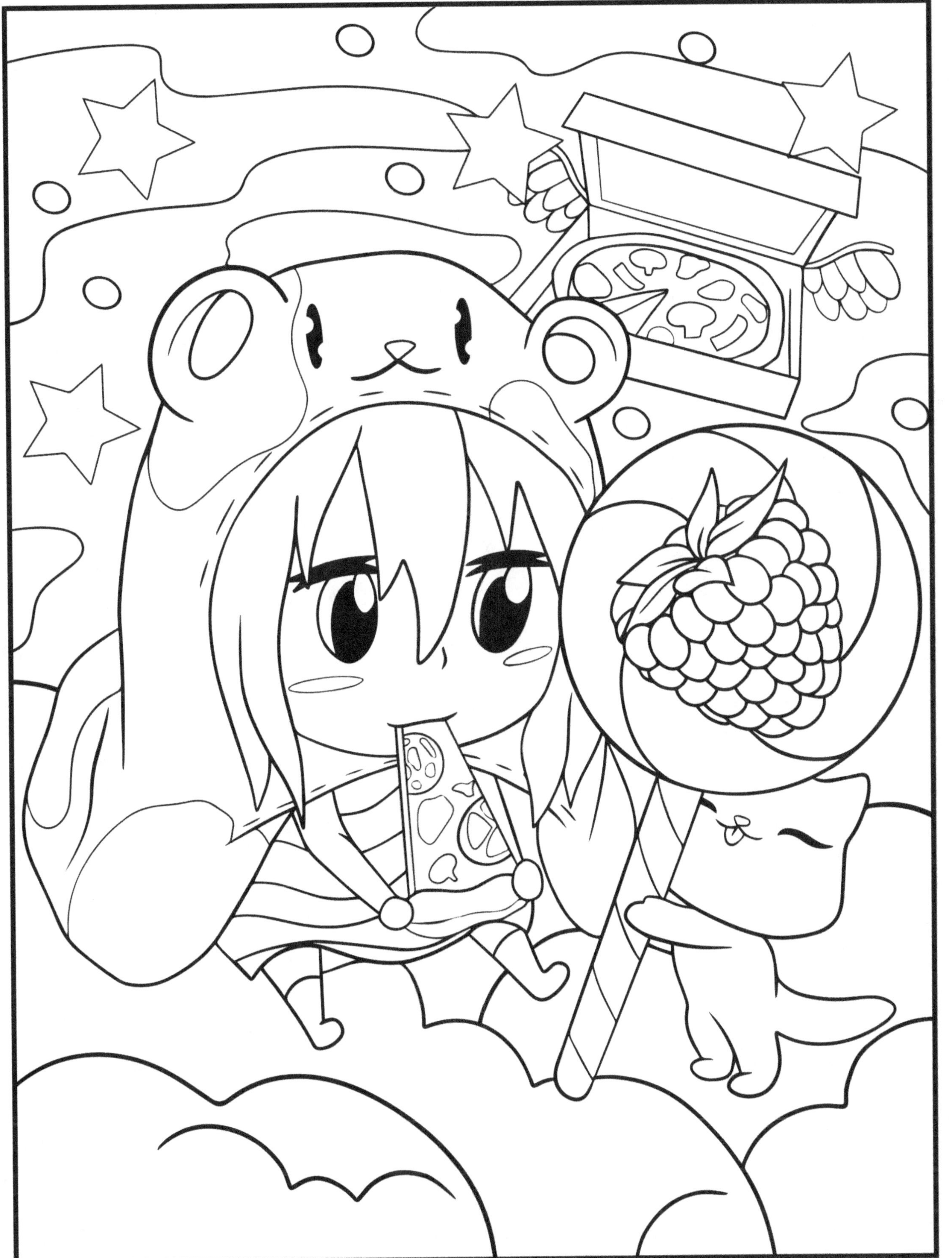

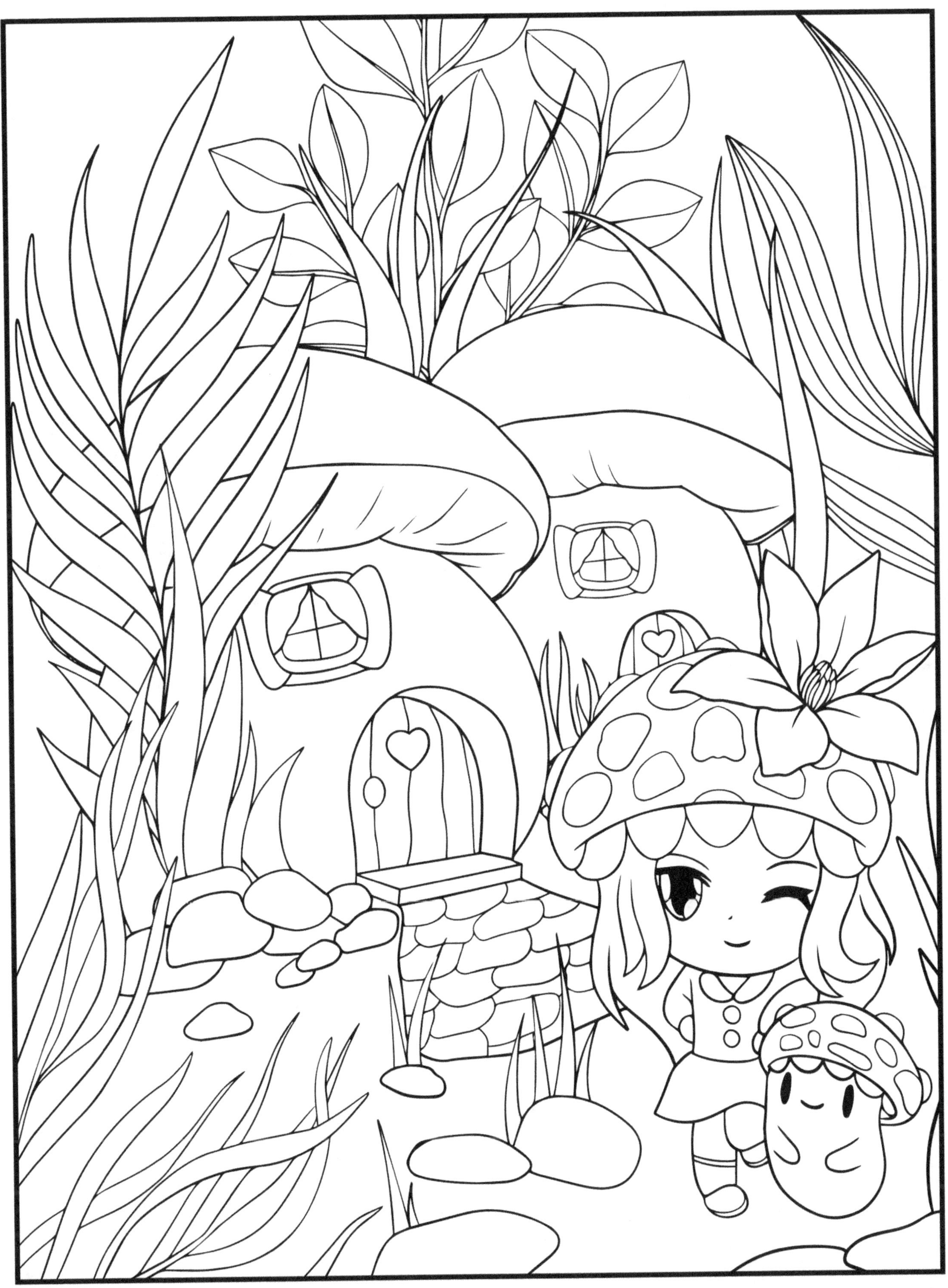

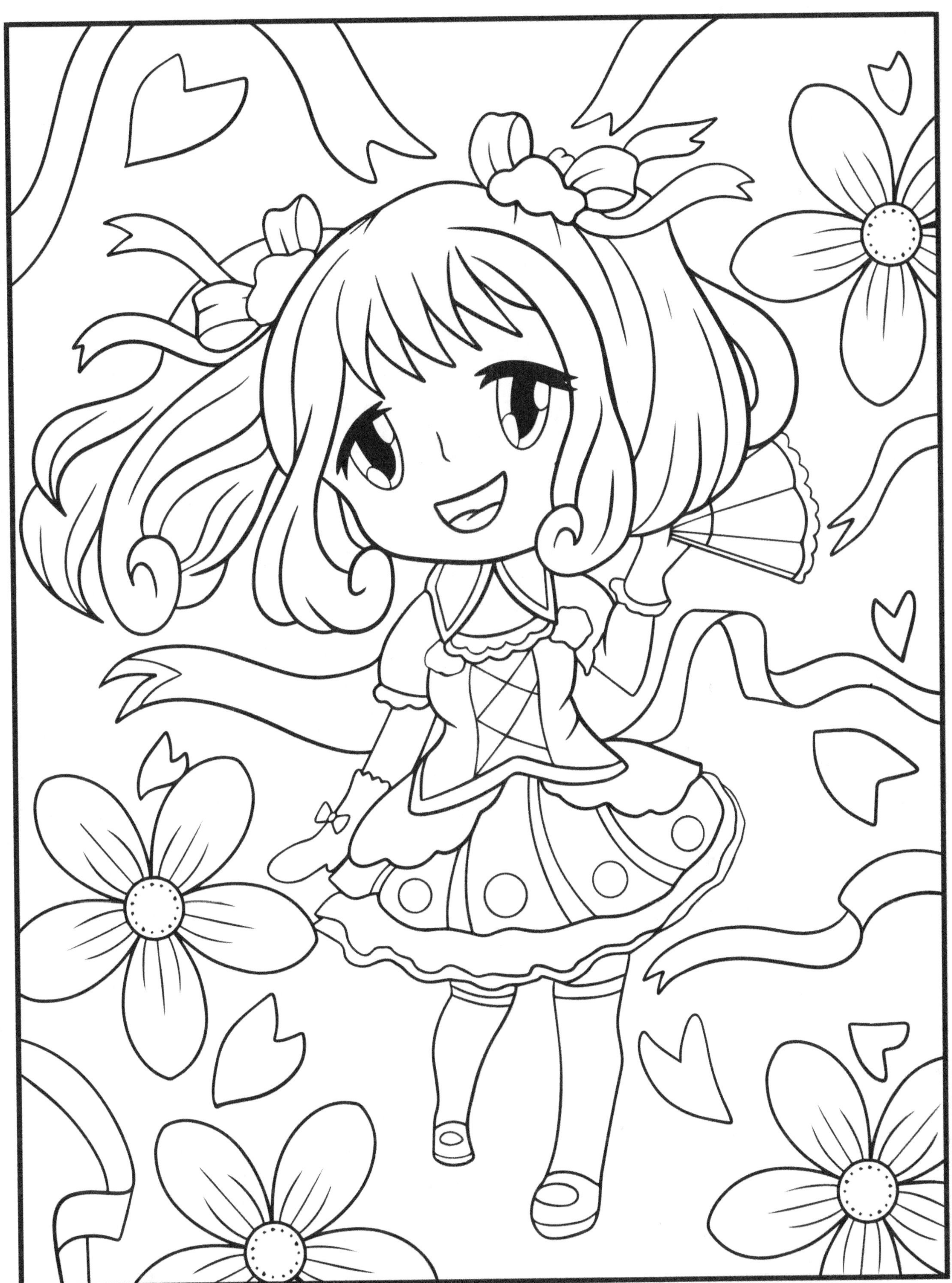

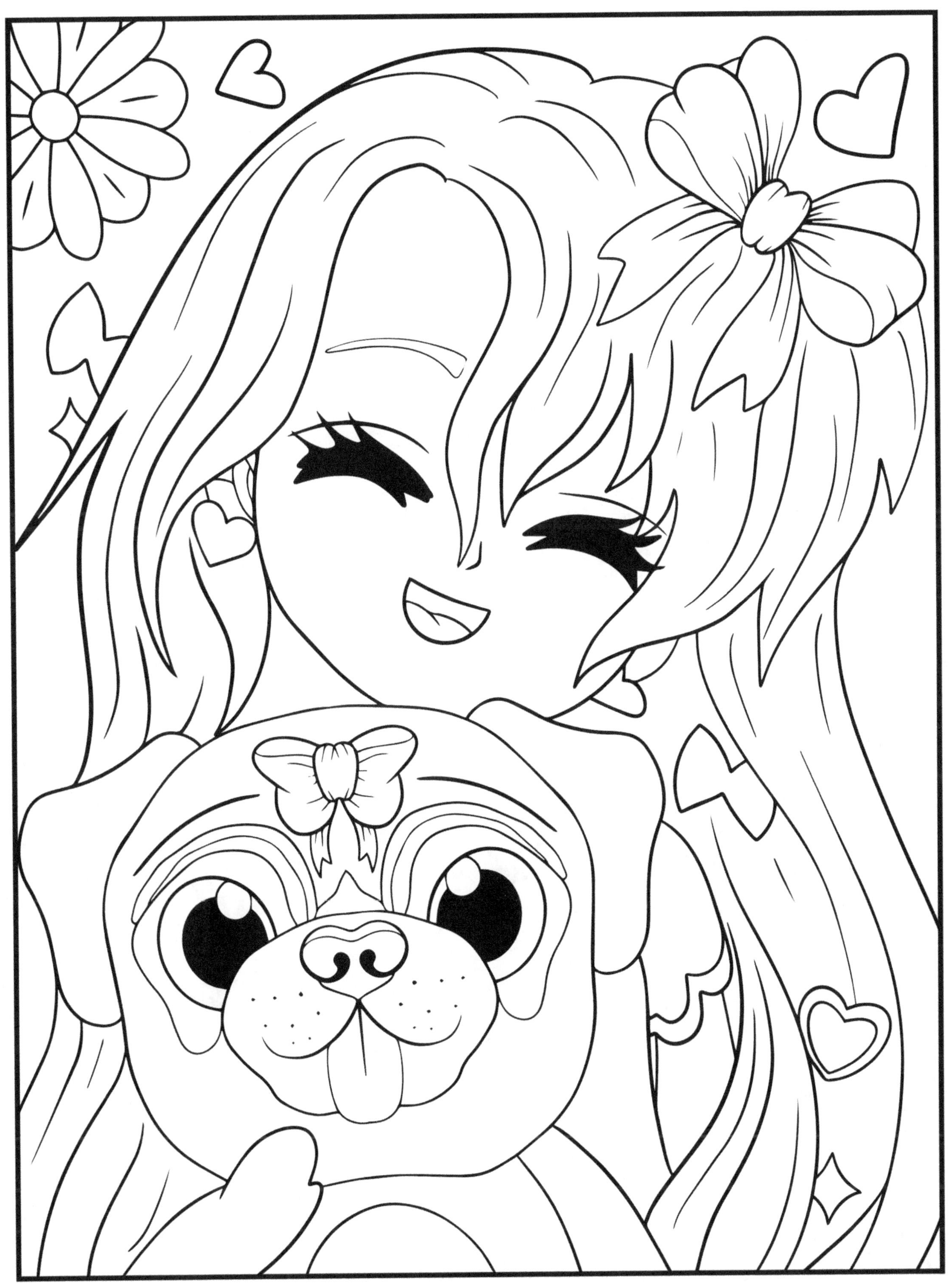

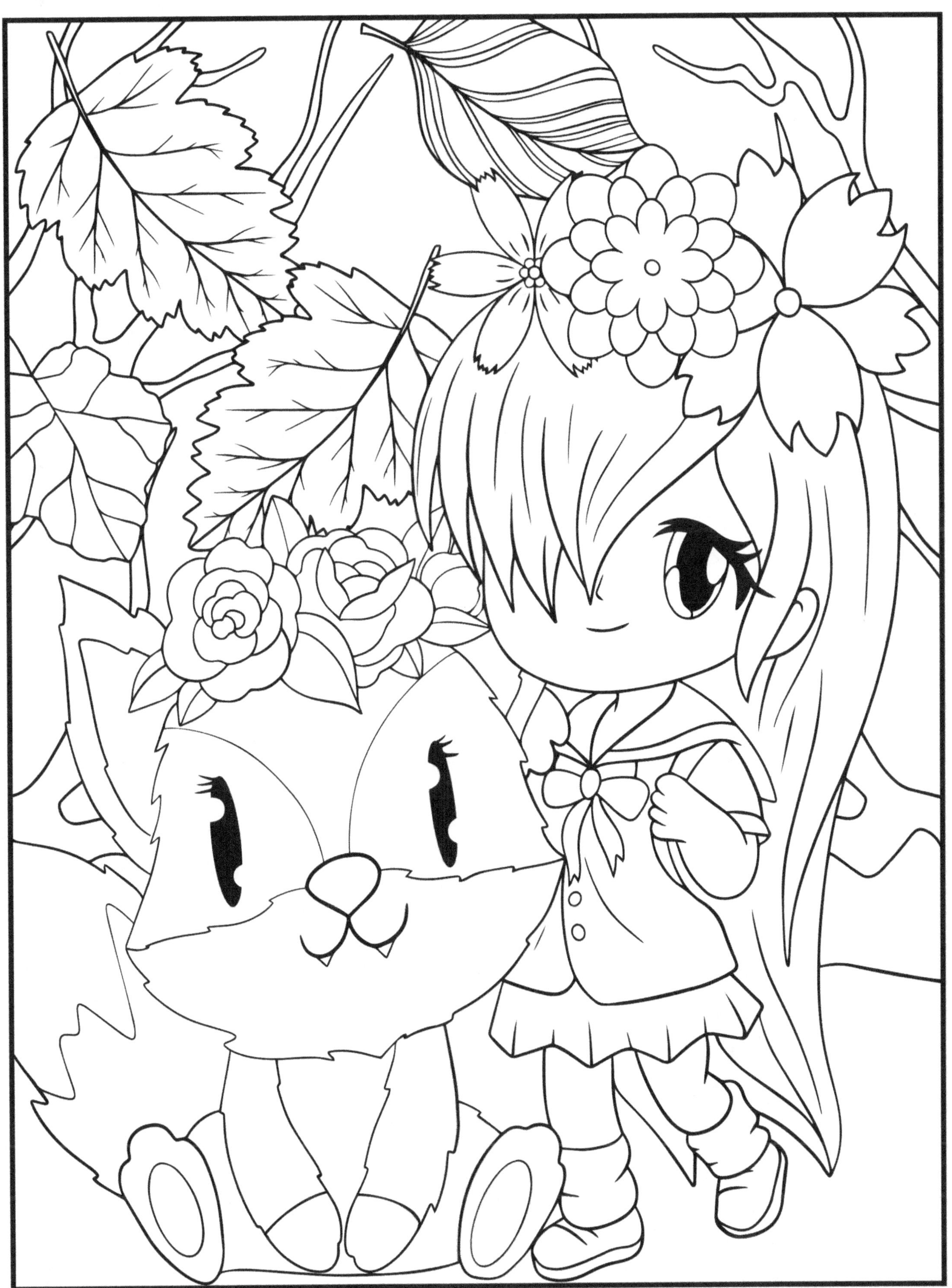

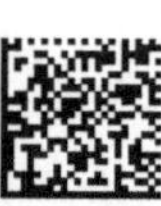